The Structure
of the Body

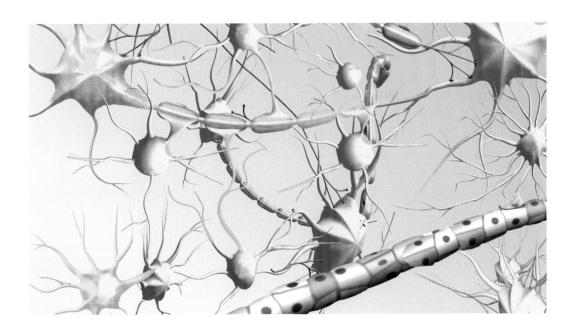

WORLD ALMANAC® LIBRARY

Please visit our web site at: www.worldalmanaclibrary.com
For a free color catalog describing World Almanac® Library's list of high-quality books and
multimedia programs, call 1-800-848-2928 or fax your request to (414) 332-3567.

The editors at World Almanac® Library would like to thank Dr. Ron Gerrits, Professor of Biomedical
Engineering, Milwaukee School of Engineering, for the technical expertise and advice he brought to the
production of this book.

Library of Congress Cataloging-in-Publication Data

The structure of the body.
  p. cm. — (21st century science)
  Summary: Describes the various parts of the human body and how they carry out their specific functions.
  Includes bibliographical references and index.
  ISBN 0-8368-5008-4 (lib. bdg.)
  1. Body, Human—Juvenile literature. 2. Human anatomy—Juvenile literature. 3. Human physiology—
Juvenile literature. [1. Body, Human. 2. Human anatomy. 3. Physiology.] I. Title. II. Series.
QM27.S77   2002
  611—dc21   2002022704

This North American edition first published in 2002 by
World Almanac® Library
330 West Olive Street, Suite 100
Milwaukee, WI 53212 USA

Created and produced as *The human body* by
QA INTERNATIONAL
329 rue de la Commune Ouest, 3ᵉ étage
Montreal, Québec
Canada H2Y 2E1
Tel: (514) 499-3000 Fax: (514) 499-3010
www.qa-international.com

© QA International, 2002

Publisher: Jacques Fortin

Editorial Director: François Fortin

Executive Directors: Stéphane Batigne, Serge D'Amico

Illustrations Editor: Marc Lalumière

Art Director: Rielle Lévesque

Graphic Designer: Anne Tremblay

Writers: Stéphane Batigne, Josée Bourbonnière, Nathalie Fredette

Computer Graphic Artists: Jean-Yves Ahern, Pierre Beauchemin, Maxime Bigras, Yan Bohler, Mélanie
Boivin, Jocelyn Gardner, Danièle Lemay, Alain Lemire, Raymond Martin, Annie Maurice, Anouk Noël,
Carl Pelletier, Simon Pelletier, Claude Thivierge, Michel Rouleau, Frédérick Simard

Page Layout: Véronique Boisvert, Geneviève Théroux Béliveau

Researchers: Kathleen Wynd, Jessie Daigle, Anne-Marie Villeneuve

Copy Editor: Jane Broderick

Translation: Käthe Roth

Production: Mac Thien Nguyen Hoang

Prepress: Tony O'Riley

Reviewers: Dr. Alain Beaudet (Department of Neurology and Neurosurgery, McGill University), Dr. Amanda Black
(Department of Obstetrics and Gynaecology, Queen's University), Dr. Richard Cloutier (Département de dermatologie,
Centre hospitalier universitaire de Québec), Dr. Luisa Deutsch (KGK Synergize), Dr. René Dinh, Dr. Annie Goyette
(Département d'ophtalmologie, Centre hospitalier universitaire de Québec), Dr. Pierre Duguay, Dr. Vincent Gracco
(School of Communication Sciences and Disorders, Faculty of Medicine, McGill University), Dr. Pierre Guy (Orthopedic
Trauma Service, McGill University Health Centre), Dr. Michael Hawke (Department of Otolaryngology, Faculty of
Medicine, University of Toronto), Dr. Patrice Hugo, Dr. Ann-Muriel Steff (Procrea BioSciences Inc.), Dr. Roman
Jednak (Division of Urology, The Montreal Children's Hospital), Dr. Michael S. Kramer (Departments of Pediatrics and
of Epidemiology and Biostatistics, Faculty of Medicine, McGill University), Dr. Pierre Lachapelle (Department of
Ophthalmology, McGill University), Dr. Denis Laflamme, Dr. Maria Do Carmo (MD Multimedia Inc.), Dr. Claude
Lamarche (Faculté de médecine dentaire, Université de Montréal), Dr. Sheldon Magder (Faculty of Medicine, McGill
University), Dr. Nelson Nadeau, Dr. Louis Z. G. Touyz (Faculty of Dentistry, McGill University), Dr. Teresa
Trippenbach (Department of Physiology, McGill University), Dr. Martine Turcotte, Dr. Michael Wiseman (Faculty of
Dentistry, McGill University).

World Almanac® Library Editor: Alan Wachtel

World Almanac® Library Art Direction: Tammy Gruenewald

Cover Design: Katherine A. Goedheer

Printed in Canada

1 2 3 4 5 6 7 8 9 06 05 04 03 02

Table of Contents

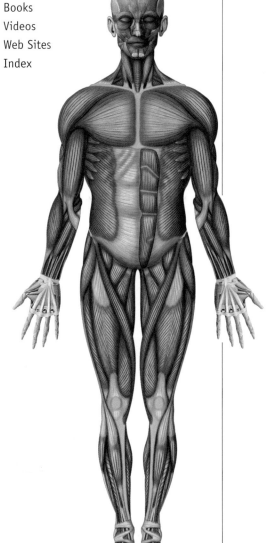

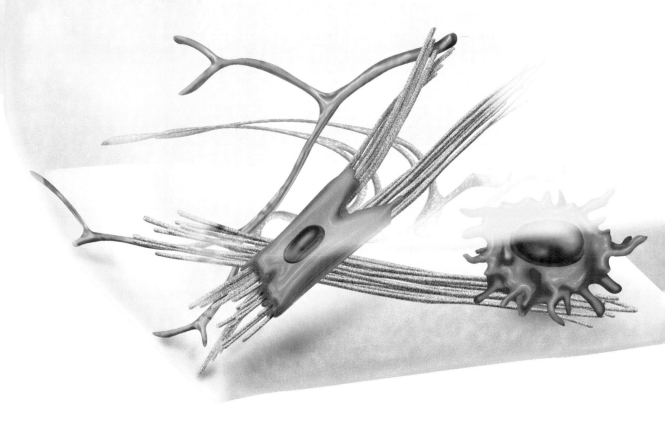

What is the human body made of? Although our bodies are very complex, they are composed of fundamental units, called cells, that are very similar to each other. These microscopic basic components assemble to form the different tissues that make up all the body's organs. Cells are the sites of intense and constant activity; they manufacture living matter, consume energy, and continually reproduce themselves.

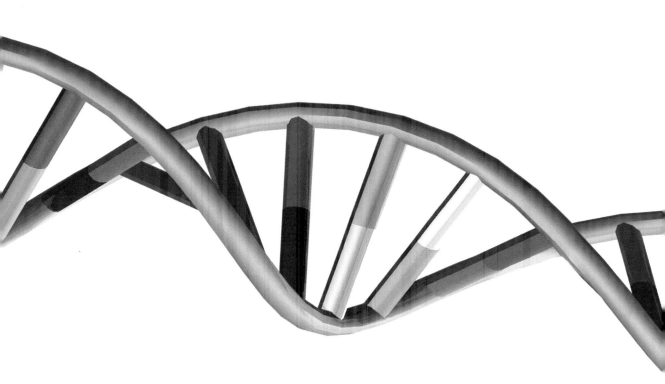

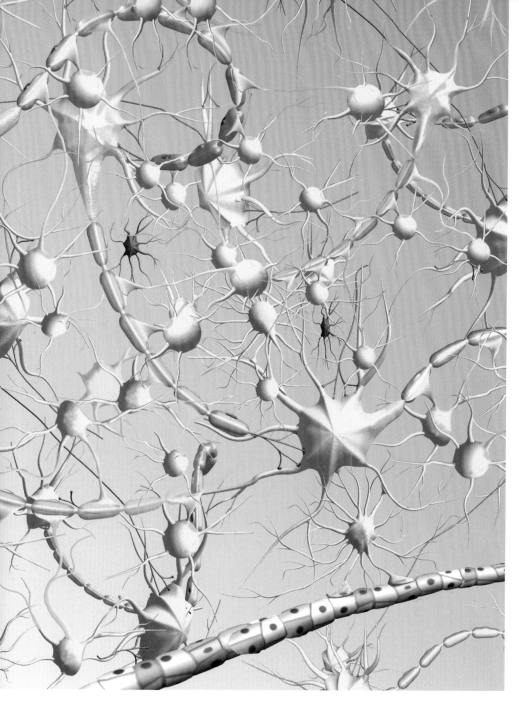

The Body's Building Blocks

The Human Cell
The body's basic component

The human body contains about 60 billion cells. Since a cell's diameter is generally less than a few hundredths of a millimeter, these basic components of the human body are invisible to the naked eye. Although they can take many different shapes depending on their location and function, all human cells have the same well-defined structure consisting of an exterior membrane, a nucleus, and several internal elements floating in a gelatinous medium called cytoplasm.

DIFFERENT TYPES OF CELLS

The human body contains many types of cells, which are differentiated according to their functions. Despite their different sizes and shapes, all have the same general structure.

The **cones** of the retina contain light-sensitive pigments.

The nucleus of a **neutrophil** has several lobes.

Erythrocytes, or red blood cells, color the blood red.

Ova are the largest human cells.

Spermatozoa have a long flagellum.

Neurons, or nerve cells, can be over 3 feet (1 meter) long.

The irregular shapes of **osteocytes**, or bone cells, enable them to lodge in very narrow cavities of bony tissue.

Cytoplasm, which fills the intracellular space, is a jelly-like substance composed of water, proteins, lipids, ions, and glucose.

Lysosomes contain enzymes that perform intracellular digestion.

Microtubules, which are the supporting structure of the cell, make it easier for organelles to move around within the cytoplasm.

Made mainly of lipid molecules, the **cell membrane** is a selective, water-insoluble barrier.

Enveloped in double membranes, **mitochondria** produce and store energy.

Enzymes in **peroxisomes** perform oxidization.

Cilia, formed of groups of microtubules covered by the cellular membrane, can propel the cell or move substances outside the cell. Large cilia are called flagella.

THE STRUCTURE OF HUMAN CELLS

Human cells, like the cells of all higher-order life forms, are eukaryotes—that is, their genetic material is enclosed in a nucleus surrounded by a nuclear membrane. The rest of the cell is filled with cytoplasm, a semi-liquid medium structured by a network of microtubules and microfilaments. The **organelles** that float in the cytoplasm—including mitochondria, the Golgi apparatus, the endoplasmic reticulum, and lysosomes—perform different functions within the cell, such as storing energy, synthesizing and transporting proteins, and digesting foreign bodies.

Chromatin, the main component of the nucleus, is a filament formed of DNA and proteins.

The **nuclear membrane** has a large number of pores.

free ribosome

Ribosomes are made in the **nucleolus**, the center of the nucleus.

The **endoplasmic reticulum**, or ER, which is located near the nucleus, consists of a network of membranous pockets and canals. The part called the rough ER is covered with ribosomes that synthesize proteins, while the section called the smooth ER does not have ribosomes and synthesizes other substances.

The **Golgi apparatus** resembles a series of membranous sacs attached to the rough ER. It collects the proteins synthesized by the ribosomes, sometimes changes them by adding carbohydrates, then releases them into vacuoles.

Microfilaments are made of a protein called actin. Along with microtubules, they form the cytoskeleton that gives a cell its shape.

Vacuoles are the small, liquid-filled vesicles that transport proteins from the Golgi apparatus to the edge of the cellular membrane, where the proteins are released.

TRANSPORT OF PROTEINS IN THE CELL

Protein synthesis, one of the main functions of cells, is performed on small organelles called **ribosomes**. There are two types of ribosomes: free ribosomes, which release their products directly into the cytoplasm, and ribosomes attached to the endoplasmic reticulum, which make proteins that are released outside the cell. Proteins made by the second type of ribosomes move through the network of membranous sacs in the endoplasmic reticulum, are processed by the Golgi apparatus, and then migrate inside a vacuole toward the cellular membrane.

Each cell has two **centrioles** that are made of bundles of microtubules at a right angle to each other. They play a role in cell division.

DNA and Chromosomes

The code of life deep within cells

Most cells in our bodies have a nucleus. Although nuclei are only a few microns in diameter, they contain the instructions for all of the cell's processes. The substance in which these important instructions are stored is deoxyribonucleic acid, better known as DNA.

DNA takes the form of very long, helical molecules. DNA molecules are unique in that they are made of two strands linked by several billion successive bonds between nucleotides. The sequence of these bonds constitutes a code that commands the production of a large number of specific proteins and also the replication of itself.

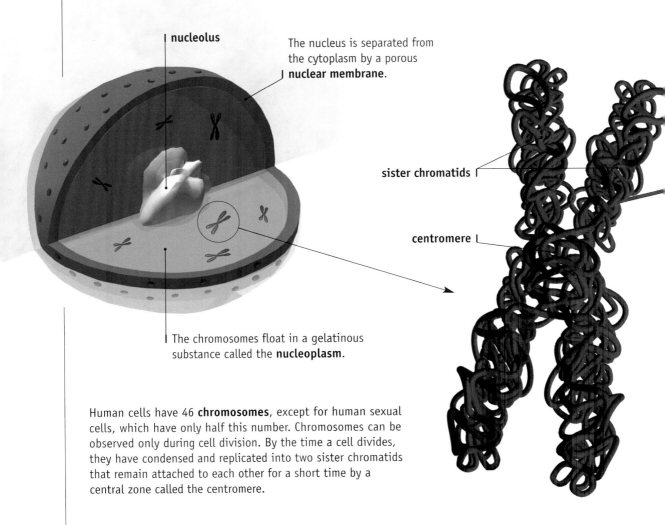

nucleolus

The nucleus is separated from the cytoplasm by a porous **nuclear membrane**.

sister chromatids

centromere

The chromosomes float in a gelatinous substance called the **nucleoplasm**.

Human cells have 46 **chromosomes**, except for human sexual cells, which have only half this number. Chromosomes can be observed only during cell division. By the time a cell divides, they have condensed and replicated into two sister chromatids that remain attached to each other for a short time by a central zone called the centromere.

INSIDE THE NUCLEUS

With the exception of mature red blood cells, all cells in the body contain a nucleus. Some, like muscle cells, even have several nuclei. The nucleus of a cell contains one or more nucleoli and filaments of chromatin floating in its nucleoplasm. A filament of chromatin, which generally looks like a string of beads, is composed of a long DNA molecule wound around proteins called histones. When a cell divides, these filaments roll up into spirals, become condensed, and organize into small rods called chromosomes.

THE MOLECULAR STRUCTURE OF DNA

DNA molecules are polymers—that is, they are complex molecules composed of a large number of simpler molecules. The structure of a DNA molecule can be visualized as a very long, twisted ladder whose two uprights are linked by billions of rungs, each of which is composed of two smaller molecules called nitrogenous bases. There are only four different kinds of nitrogenous bases in DNA: adenine, thymine, cytosine, and guanine. These molecules link up according to a strict rule that is a result of their respective molecular structures: adenine can link only with thymine, and cytosine only with guanine. The nitrogenous bases that can link up with one another are said to be complementary.

The **nucleotide** is the basic component of the DNA molecule. It is composed of a phosphate group and deoxyribose, a sugar, to which one of the four bases attaches.

Adenine can link up only with thymine.

deoxyribose

phosphate group

thymine

The **nitrogenous base**, attached to deoxyribose, bonds with its complementary base to form a rung in the DNA molecule.

guanine

Cytosine is the complementary base for guanine.

chromatin

Each chromosome has a single **DNA molecule**, .00000008 inch (.000002 millimeter) wide but several inches long.

GENETIC HERITAGE AND HEREDITY

All of the cells in an individual's body have resulted from the division of a single initial cell; thus, they all contain absolutely identical DNA filaments. From one human being to another, however, the sequence of nitrogenous bases is almost always different; the DNA structure of a human is usually unique. Identical twins are the only exceptions.

Much of our genetic heritage is linked to our belonging to the human race; all humans, for instance, have the same internal organs. Other more specific genetic characteristics— including physical features and tendencies to get certain diseases—are transmitted from one generation to the next through DNA during fertilization. This transmission of characteristics is called heredity.

When the DNA molecule wraps around eight histone molecules, it forms a mass called a **nucleosome** that supports it.

Cellular Activity

Cell division and protein synthesis

Like the more complex living organisms they make up, the cells in our bodies are born and die. Different kinds of cells have very different life spans. For example, white blood cells sometimes live only for a few hours, while red blood cells can live for four months. When they die, most cells are replaced by identical cells. A cell's life is can be described as a cycle during which it prepares for and completes its reproduction by cellular division.

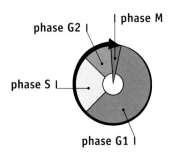

phase M

phase G2

phase S

phase G1

The **cell cycle** consists of four successive stages: three phases of interphase—called phases G1, S, and G2—and phase M. Phases G1 and G2 are times of intense metabolic activity and growth. G1 is the longest phase and the one most variable in length, lasting from 10 hours to the entire life span of the cell, depending on the kind of cell. Phase G2 lasts one to two hours. Phase S, which can last between four and eight hours, is the period during which replication of DNA takes place. Phase M corresponds to cell division itself and lasts only a few minutes.

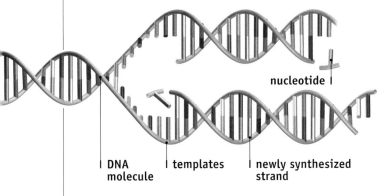

nucleotide

DNA molecule

templates

newly synthesized strand

REPLICATION OF DNA

Replication of DNA, or the copying of a cell's genetic material, is an essential step in cell division. For this replication to occur, the two strands of the double helix separate and become templates for the synthesis of two new strands, formed according to the rules of bonding between bases. When the DNA molecule has completely replicated, the cell has two absolutely identical molecules.

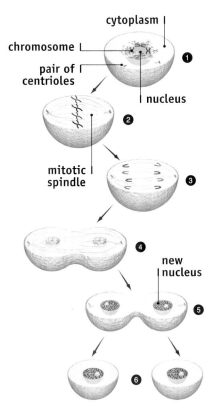

cytoplasm

chromosome

pair of centrioles

nucleus

mitotic spindle

new nucleus

CELL DIVISION

The process of cell division, also known as mitosis, includes several distinct steps. The DNA molecules, which are in the form of chromatin during interphase, coil and thicken during prophase ❶, which makes the chromosomes visible. The nucleolus disappears and the two centrioles move apart and migrate to opposite ends of the cell, while a system of microfilaments called the mitotic spindle forms between these two poles. Gradually, the nuclear membrane disintegrates and the chromosomes move along the filaments of the mitotic spindle. During metaphase ❷, the chromosomes line up at the center of the cell. When their centromeres divide, anaphase begins ❸. The chromatids, which have become complete chromosomes, are drawn to one or the other end of the cell. In telophase ❹, a new nucleus forms at each end of the cell. The chromosomes uncoil to become chromatin once more, while a new nuclear membrane is formed. The mitotic spindle disappears and the cytoplasm begins to separate during a phase called cytokinesis ❺. At the end of the process, the original cell is replaced by two identical new cells ❻.

SYNTHESIS OF PROTEINS

Proteins are large molecules formed by the linking together of many amino acids. Some proteins—for example, hormones, antibodies, and enzymes—play specific roles in the body's functioning, while others constitute its living material. The synthesis of proteins, which is one of the cell's main functions, is performed according to instructions coded in **genes**, or different sequences of nitrogenous bases along segments of a DNA molecule. Each gene has its own particular sequence of nitrogenous bases. The synthesis of a protein requires transcribing this sequence onto a messenger molecule and then translating it into the sequence of amino acids that form the protein.

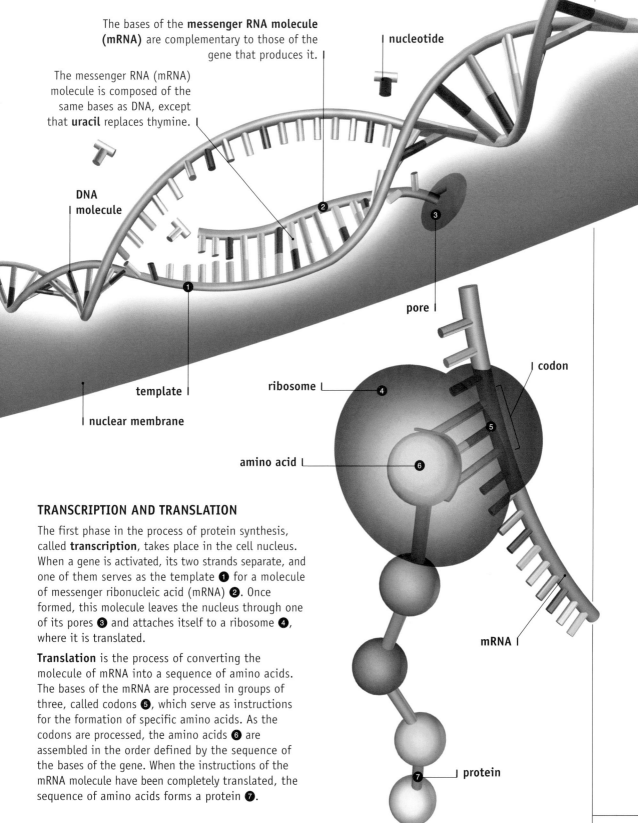

The bases of the **messenger RNA molecule (mRNA)** are complementary to those of the gene that produces it.

The messenger RNA (mRNA) molecule is composed of the same bases as DNA, except that **uracil** replaces thymine.

nucleotide

DNA molecule

pore

ribosome

codon

template

amino acid

nuclear membrane

mRNA

protein

TRANSCRIPTION AND TRANSLATION

The first phase in the process of protein synthesis, called **transcription**, takes place in the cell nucleus. When a gene is activated, its two strands separate, and one of them serves as the template ❶ for a molecule of messenger ribonucleic acid (mRNA) ❷. Once formed, this molecule leaves the nucleus through one of its pores ❸ and attaches itself to a ribosome ❹, where it is translated.

Translation is the process of converting the molecule of mRNA into a sequence of amino acids. The bases of the mRNA are processed in groups of three, called codons ❺, which serve as instructions for the formation of specific amino acids. As the codons are processed, the amino acids ❻ are assembled in the order defined by the sequence of the bases of the gene. When the instructions of the mRNA molecule have been completely translated, the sequence of amino acids forms a protein ❼.

Body Tissues

In the human body, cells do not function separately. They are grouped together in the different kinds of tissues that compose a person's organs. There are four types of tissues in the human body: epithelial tissues, which cover many parts of the body; muscle tissues, which contract to move parts of the body; nerve tissues, which carry nerve impulses; and connective tissues, which surround and support other tissues. Aside from cells, tissues contain extracellular liquid in which substances needed by the body, such as hormones, proteins, and vitamins, circulate and dissolve.

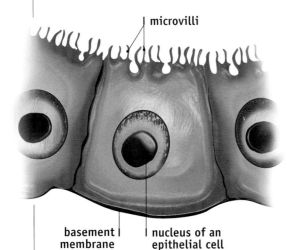

microvilli

basement membrane

nucleus of an epithelial cell

EPITHELIAL TISSUE

Epithelial tissue is the name for the kind of tissue that covers most of the internal and external surfaces of the body. Skin, blood vessels, glands, and the cavities of the digestive system are made of epithelial tissue. Epithelial cells are either cuboidal, columnar, or squamous (flat) in shape and are tightly packed against each other to form coverings that can have one or more layers. These coverings sit on a basement membrane that connects to underlying vascularized tissue. Epithelial tissues found on the outside of the body are impermeable to most substances, but those on the inside play a role of absorption and secretion within the organism, due to the microvilli that cover them.

CONNECTIVE TISSUE

Cartilage, bony tissue, blood, and many of the tissues that make up the body's organs are connective tissues. Connective tissue has relatively few cells compared to epithelial tissue. Its cells float in a very abundant intercellular matrix composed mainly of fibers and a semiliquid substance. Connective tissue cells fall into two main categories: fibroblasts and macrophages. Fibroblasts secrete collagen fibers, elastic fibers, and reticular fibers, all of which are composed of proteins and are important components of connective tissues. The density and positioning of these fibers, as well as the presence of other, more specific, cells gives different types of connective tissues very different properties.

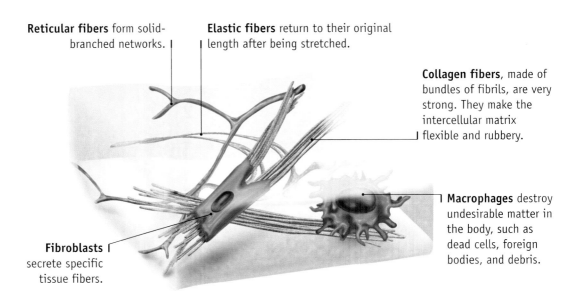

Reticular fibers form solid-branched networks.

Elastic fibers return to their original length after being stretched.

Collagen fibers, made of bundles of fibrils, are very strong. They make the intercellular matrix flexible and rubbery.

Macrophages destroy undesirable matter in the body, such as dead cells, foreign bodies, and debris.

Fibroblasts secrete specific tissue fibers.

MUSCLE TISSUE

Muscle tissues are distinguished by the way their cells are bundled. The three types of muscle tissue are skeletal muscle, cardiac muscle, and smooth muscle.

Muscle cells are called **fibers**, but they should not be confused with the fibers present in connective tissue.

cell nucleus

Skeletal muscle tissue is formed of very elongated multinucleated fibers. These cells look striated due to the alternation of the two types of filaments that compose them.

The fibers of **cardiac muscle tissue** are also striated, but this type of tissue has a different pattern of fibers than skeletal muscle.

Smooth muscle tissue is made up of shorter, spindle-shaped cells. These fibers have only one nucleus and are not striated.

NERVE TISSUE

The brain, the spinal cord, and the nerves are formed of nerve tissue, which consists of a dense tangle of cells. The two categories of cells that make up nerve tissue are neurons and glial cells. Neurons are the true nervous cells because they carry nerve impulses. Glial cells, including astrocytes, oligodendrocytes, microglia, Schwann cells, and others, are generally smaller than neurons and ten times more numerous. They support, protect, and nourish neurons but do not play a direct role in nerve functions. Unlike neurons, they are capable of dividing by mitosis.

Neurons are highly specialized cells that transport and transmit nerve impulses by establishing countless connections between each other.

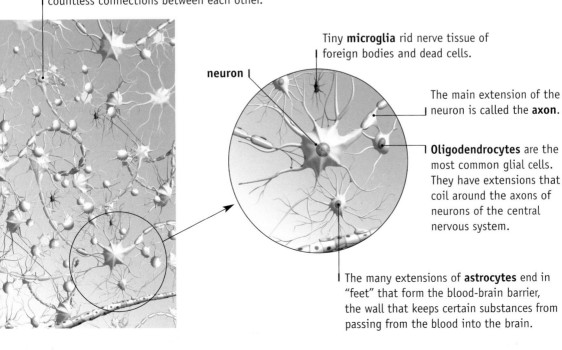

Tiny **microglia** rid nerve tissue of foreign bodies and dead cells.

neuron

The main extension of the neuron is called the **axon**.

Oligodendrocytes are the most common glial cells. They have extensions that coil around the axons of neurons of the central nervous system.

The many extensions of **astrocytes** end in "feet" that form the blood-brain barrier, the wall that keeps certain substances from passing from the blood into the brain.

From the phalanges to the bones of the skull, the 206 bones that make up the human skeleton play essential supportive and protective roles in the architecture of the body. But the structure of the human body does not consist solely of its skeleton. We also have more than 600 muscles with which we control our limbs and move around. This strong, efficient internal structure could not function without the protective envelope that covers it—the skin.

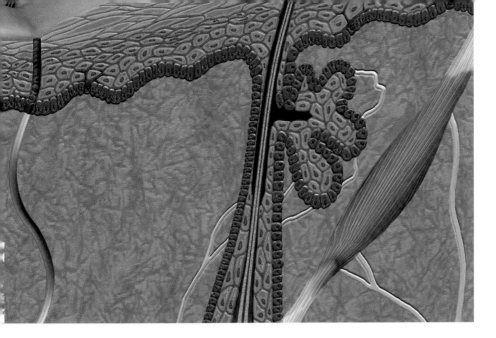

The Architecture of the Body

The Skin

The body's protective envelope

We may not often think of it this way, but the skin is the largest organ of the human body; an adult's skin covers almost 19 square feet (1.75 square meters) and contributes 7 percent of total body mass. This covering has a superficial layer, the epidermis, and a deeper layer, the dermis. With the different types of cells that it contains, including keratinocytes, melanocytes, and sensory receptors, the skin protects us from the external environment in many ways.

THE LAYERS OF THE EPIDERMIS

The epidermis is an epithelial tissue that has several layers and is made mainly of keratinocytes. These cells form in the deepest layer of the epidermis, or the basal layer, and then are pushed up toward the spiny layer by younger cells. As they migrate, the keratinocytes are impregnated with a fibrous protein called keratin that gradually replaces their cytoplasm. By the time the cells reach the outer layer of the epidermis, called the hornlike layer, their nuclei have completely disintegrated. These dead, flattened keratinous cells make the skin impermeable to most substances.

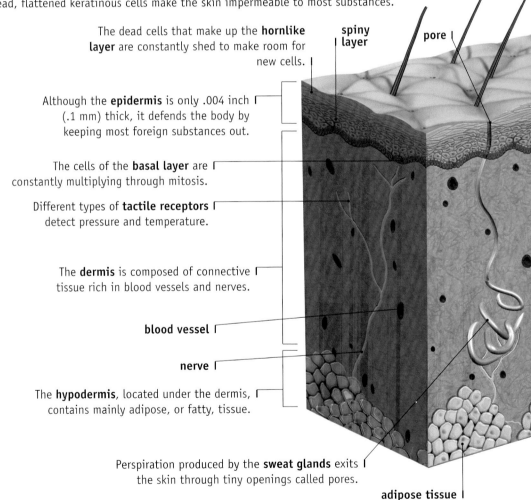

The dead cells that make up the **hornlike layer** are constantly shed to make room for new cells.

spiny layer

pore

Although the **epidermis** is only .004 inch (.1 mm) thick, it defends the body by keeping most foreign substances out.

The cells of the **basal layer** are constantly multiplying through mitosis.

Different types of **tactile receptors** detect pressure and temperature.

The **dermis** is composed of connective tissue rich in blood vessels and nerves.

blood vessel

nerve

The **hypodermis**, located under the dermis, contains mainly adipose, or fatty, tissue.

Perspiration produced by the **sweat glands** exits the skin through tiny openings called pores.

adipose tissue

THE SKIN'S DEFENSES

Human skin has many features that protect the body against various assaults. The epidermis contains the proteins keratin and melanin; keratin makes it impermeable to most substances, while melanin blocks out some ultraviolet rays that can burn it. Perspiration protects the body against certain bacteria, cools the skin, and evacuates certain substances. Sebum, released by sebaceous glands attached to hair follicles, is a fatty substance that protects the skin from bacteria and keeps it from drying out. Sensory receptors in the skin detect injuries to the body, making it possible for the central nervous system to react.

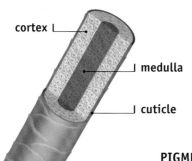

cortex
medulla
cuticle

Hair, which sprouts from the hair follicles in the dermis, grows over most of our skin. Hair follicles have sebaceous glands, which coat hairs with sebum; arrector pili muscles, which pull them upright when one is cold or scared; and nerve receptors, which can detect even very light touches.

PIGMENTS FOR SUN PROTECTION

The deepest layer of the epidermis contains specialized cells called melanocytes. Activated by the melanocyte-stimulating hormone made by the pituitary gland, melanocytes produce melanin, a dark-brown pigment. Melanin molecules released by the cellular extensions of melanocytes enter the keratinocytes and settle over cell nuclei to give them some protection from potentially carcinogenic ultraviolet rays.

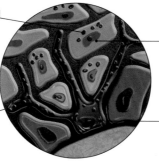

melanin

keratinocyte

Melanocytes make up 8 percent of the cells of the epidermis. The color of the skin depends not on the number of melanocytes but on their size and amount of activity.

Sebaceous glands produce sebum, an oily substance that coats the hairs and skin.

arrector pili muscle

hair follicle

HOW THE SKIN FORMS SCARS

When the skin is injured down to the dermis or even the hypodermis ❶, a substance generated by blood coagulation, called fibrin, rapidly forms a clot at the bottom of the wound ❷. When the clot dries up, it creates a crust ❸ that has to be eliminated in order for the cells of the basal layer of the epidermis to migrate to form new skin. At the same time, fibroblasts ❹ and capillaries, or small blood vessels, of the dermis multiply to reconstruct the tissue ❺. As new tissue grows, it pushes the crust toward the surface of the epidermis, where a small swelling, or scar, may form ❻.

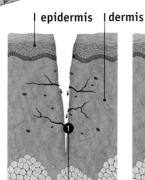
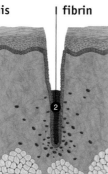
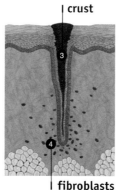
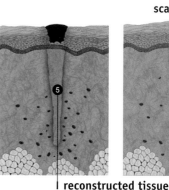
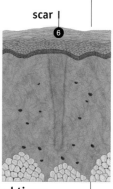

epidermis | dermis | fibrin | crust | scar

deep wound | fibroblasts | reconstructed tissue

Bone Structure

Flexible yet strong tissues

A bone is six times as strong as a bar of steel of the same weight. This remarkable strength comes from the structure of bony tissues. The different types of bones in the body are all made of both compact bone tissue and spongy, or cancellous, bone tissue in different proportions and positions. Bony tissues contain collagen, a protein that gives bones their flexibility, and the mineral salts calcium and phosphorus, which are responsible for their solidity.

Long bones, such as the femur, have a hollow cylindrical central portion, called the shaft, and two bulges at the ends, called the epiphyses. Between the shaft and the epiphyses are the metaphyses.

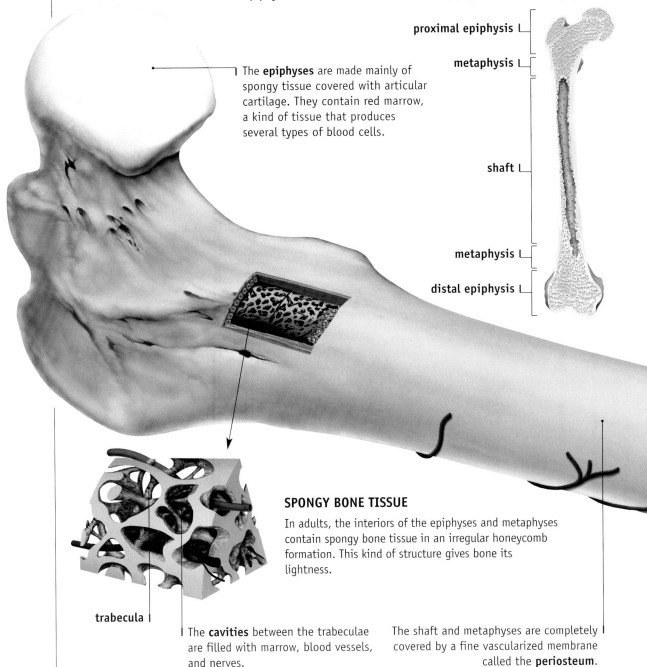

proximal epiphysis

metaphysis

The **epiphyses** are made mainly of spongy tissue covered with articular cartilage. They contain red marrow, a kind of tissue that produces several types of blood cells.

shaft

metaphysis

distal epiphysis

SPONGY BONE TISSUE

In adults, the interiors of the epiphyses and metaphyses contain spongy bone tissue in an irregular honeycomb formation. This kind of structure gives bone its lightness.

trabecula

The **cavities** between the trabeculae are filled with marrow, blood vessels, and nerves.

The shaft and metaphyses are completely covered by a fine vascularized membrane called the **periosteum**.

COMPACT BONE TISSUE

The outer layer of bones is made of compact bone tissue that is dense and remarkably resistant to pressure and shock. This tissue is composed mainly of osteons, which are small cylinders, made of concentric layers of hard matrix. Osteons are packed tightly together and connected by longitudinal canals, called haversian canals, and transversal canals, called Volkmann's canals, that contain lymphatic and blood vessels.

In spite of its density and hardness, compact bone tissue is alive. Tiny cavities, called lacunae, and canals, known as canaliculi, between the lamellae are filled with osteocytes, which are the mature bone cells responsible for providing nutrition to the bone tissue.

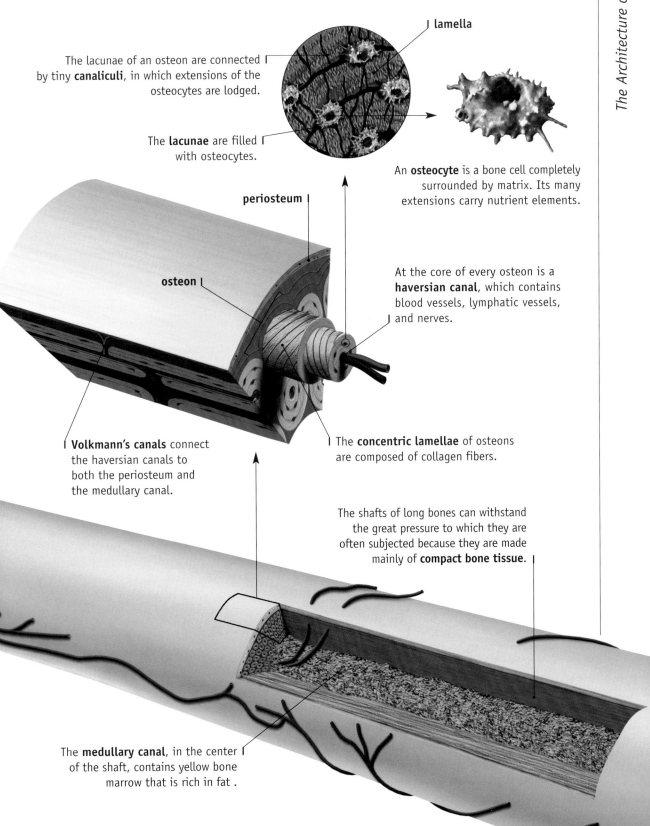

lamella

The lacunae of an osteon are connected by tiny **canaliculi**, in which extensions of the osteocytes are lodged.

The **lacunae** are filled with osteocytes.

An **osteocyte** is a bone cell completely surrounded by matrix. Its many extensions carry nutrient elements.

periosteum

osteon

At the core of every osteon is a **haversian canal**, which contains blood vessels, lymphatic vessels, and nerves.

Volkmann's canals connect the haversian canals to both the periosteum and the medullary canal.

The **concentric lamellae** of osteons are composed of collagen fibers.

The shafts of long bones can withstand the great pressure to which they are often subjected because they are made mainly of **compact bone tissue**.

The **medullary canal**, in the center of the shaft, contains yellow bone marrow that is rich in fat .

Bone Growth

From cartilage to bone tissue

Bone formation starts during the embryonic stage, but many parts of the skeleton are still made of cartilage at birth. The growth of bones continues until they reach their final size in adulthood. Their development takes place through a process, called ossification, in which cartilaginous cells multiply, die, and are replaced by bone cells.

OSSIFICATION OF CARTILAGE

A fetus' skeleton is composed of **cartilage models** that approximate the shapes of bones. Starting in the sixth week of pregnancy, cartilage cells in the centers of the cartilage models grow, explode, and die, causing calcification. At the same time, cells that produce bone tissue, known as osteoblasts, multiply on the membranes that cover the cartilage models, called perichondria.

When the fetus is about three months old, blood vessels begin to penetrate the calcified models and **primary ossification centers** appears. Osteoblasts deposit bone tissue on the calcified cartilage and form bony trabeculae. As the process extends toward the epiphyses, the trabeculae at the center of the shaft are gradually destroyed by other cells, enabling the bone to remain lightweight.

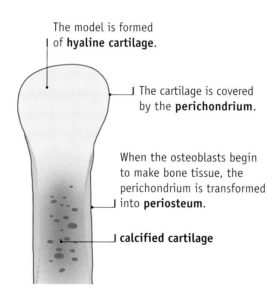

The model is formed of **hyaline cartilage**.

The cartilage is covered by the **perichondrium**.

When the osteoblasts begin to make bone tissue, the perichondrium is transformed into **periosteum**.

calcified cartilage

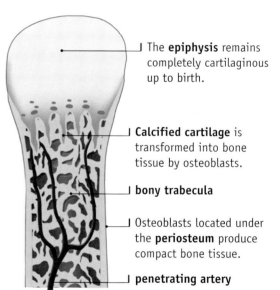

The **epiphysis** remains completely cartilaginous up to birth.

Calcified cartilage is transformed into bone tissue by osteoblasts.

bony trabecula

Osteoblasts located under the **periosteum** produce compact bone tissue.

penetrating artery

GROWTH OF THE HAND BONES

At birth ❶, the wrist is made of cartilage and the phalanges, or bones of the fingers, and the metacarpal bones, or the palms, are still incomplete. At around four years of age ❷, the carpal cartilage begins to ossify to form the wrist, while the metacarpal bones and phalanges develop. By puberty ❸, most of the bones in the wrist are formed and the bones in the palms and fingers continue to lengthen. By adulthood ❹, all the bones in the hand and wrist have finished growing.

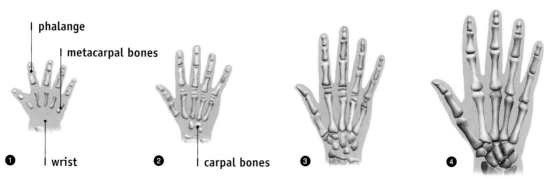

phalange

metacarpal bones

❶ wrist ❷ carpal bones ❸ ❹

At birth, a diaphysis, or shaft of a bone, has a central cavity, called the medullary canal, that is surrounded by a cylinder of compact bone tissue. Arteries penetrate the epiphyses, which causes **secondary ossification centers** to appear. The process of bone formation in the epiphyses is similar to that in a diaphysis, except that the bony trabeculae in their centers are not destroyed. Thus, instead of a medullary canal, the epiphyses contain spongy bone tissue rich in red bone marrow.

The destruction of cartilage and its replacement with bone tissue leaves a thin cartilaginous layer, known as articular cartilage, on the surface of the epiphysis. Meanwhile, the epiphysis and the shaft, or diaphysis, continue to be separated by **growth plates**. This separation allows ossification to continue and the bone to grow longer. In adulthood, this band of cartilage finally ossifies, but it remains visible as an epiphyseal line.

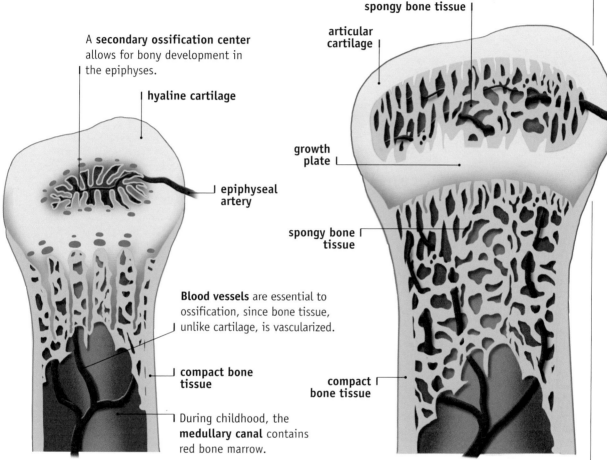

A **secondary ossification center** allows for bony development in the epiphyses.

hyaline cartilage

spongy bone tissue

articular cartilage

growth plate

epiphyseal artery

spongy bone tissue

Blood vessels are essential to ossification, since bone tissue, unlike cartilage, is vascularized.

compact bone tissue

compact bone tissue

During childhood, the **medullary canal** contains red bone marrow.

REPAIR OF A BROKEN BONE

When a bone is fractured, the blood vessels in it are also broken, and blood flows into the break. After a few hours, this blood forms a plug called a hematoma ❶. Over a few weeks, soft tissue made of specialized cells called fibroblasts and chondroblasts, known as a fibrocartilaginous callus ❷, replaces the hematoma and fuses the two parts of the bone. The fibrocartilaginous callus is gradually invaded by osteoblasts that convert it into bony callus ❸. After several months, the fractured compact bone tissue is totally reconstructed, and only a thickening ❹ of the bone remains at the site of the break.

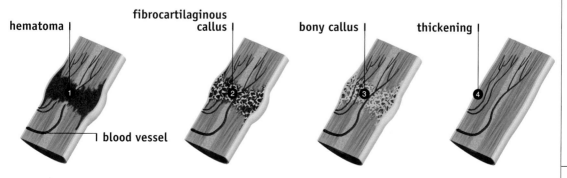

hematoma

fibrocartilaginous callus

bony callus

thickening

blood vessel

The Human Skeleton

The bony structure of the body

Like other vertebrates, human beings have an internal skeleton that supports the different muscles in the body and protects the vital organs. The positioning and articulation, or movable joining, of the bones of the skeleton also determine the kinds of movements the body can make.

The adult human skeleton usually contains 206 bones, but this number can vary slightly from individual to individual; some people, for example, have an extra pair of ribs. The bones of the human body are classified as parts of either the axial skeleton or the appendicular skeleton. The axial skeleton includes the bones of the skull, face, spine, rib cage, and sternum, while the appendicular skeleton consists of the upper limbs, lower limbs, and limb girdles—the bones of the shoulders and the hips that attach the arms and legs to the axial skeleton.

DIFFERENCES IN THE PELVIC GIRDLES OF MEN AND WOMEN

Although women's skeletons are generally smaller than men's, they are fundamentally the same in structure; only the pelvises are noticeably different. Seen from the front, a woman's pelvis is proportionally wider than a man's, though less massive. A woman's ischia are also more spread out than a man's, making her pelvic outlet—the opening formed by the bones of the pelvis and the sacrum—wider. This anatomical difference facilitates the delivery of a baby. It also changes the orientation of the acetabulum, causing differences in how men and women walk.

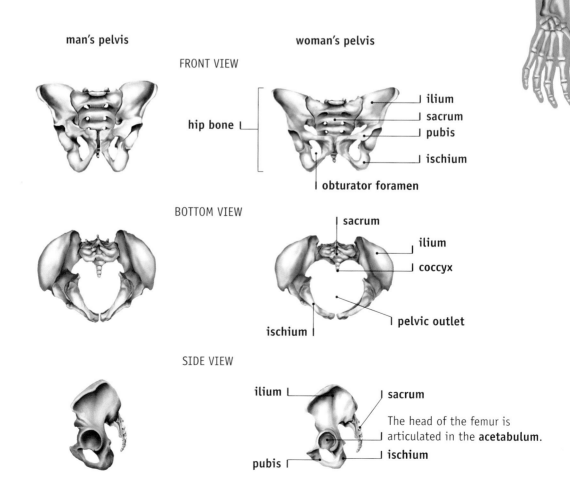

man's pelvis   woman's pelvis

FRONT VIEW

ilium
sacrum
hip bone
pubis

ischium

obturator foramen

BOTTOM VIEW

sacrum
ilium
coccyx

pelvic outlet

ischium

SIDE VIEW

ilium   sacrum

The head of the femur is articulated in the **acetabulum**.

ischium

pubis

skull

mandible

clavicle

scapula

sternum

humerus

rib cage

spine

os coxa

sacrum

ulna

radius

carpal bones

metacarpal bones

phalanges

femur

patella

tibia

fibula

tarsal bones

metatarsal bones

phalanges

THE UPPER LIMBS

The upper limbs are attached to the axial skeleton by the pectoral girdle, which consists of the scapulae, or shoulder blades, and the clavicles, or collarbones. The bone of the upper arm is called the humerus. It articulates, or joins, with the shoulder blade at the shoulder on one end. At the other end, it articulates with the bones of the forearm, the radius and ulna, to form the elbow joint.

The hand is formed of the carpal bones, which articulate with the radius at the wrist; the metacarpal bones; and the phalanges, or finger bones.

THE AXIAL SKELETON

The axial skeleton consists of 80 bones, including the bones of the skull, the spine, and the thorax. Aside from their role in protecting the vital organs—the brain, heart, lungs, and spinal cord—these bones provide the body with structure, and they support the bones of the appendicular skeleton.

THE LOWER LIMBS

The pelvis, composed of two ossa coxae and the sacrum, attaches the lower limbs to the axial skeleton. An os coxa, also called an innominate bone, results from the fusion of an ilium, a pubis, and an ischium. The pelvis also protects the organs of the pelvic cavity, which include the rectum, the bladder, and the internal genital organs.

Each leg is made up of three main bones. The femur, which articulates with the pelvis, is the longest bone in the human body. At its lower end, it forms the knee joint with the top of the tibia. This joint is protected by the patella, which is better known as the kneecap. The tibia and fibula, which together make up the lower part of the leg, are bound together by short, dense ligaments.

The foot has 26 bones. The tarsal bones structure the ankle and heel, the metatarsal bones form the sole of the foot, and the phalanges make up the toes.

Types of Bones

Form determined by function

The 206 or so bones that make up the human skeleton have a variety of shapes. There are four types of bones, classified by their general shape: long, flat, irregular, and short. This system of classification highlights the match between a bone's shape and its function.

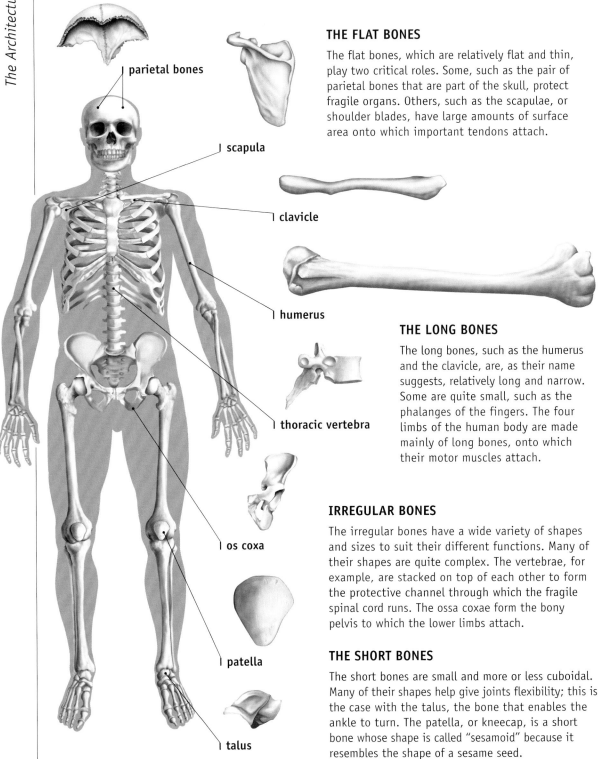

parietal bones

scapula

clavicle

humerus

thoracic vertebra

os coxa

patella

talus

THE FLAT BONES

The flat bones, which are relatively flat and thin, play two critical roles. Some, such as the pair of parietal bones that are part of the skull, protect fragile organs. Others, such as the scapulae, or shoulder blades, have large amounts of surface area onto which important tendons attach.

THE LONG BONES

The long bones, such as the humerus and the clavicle, are, as their name suggests, relatively long and narrow. Some are quite small, such as the phalanges of the fingers. The four limbs of the human body are made mainly of long bones, onto which their motor muscles attach.

IRREGULAR BONES

The irregular bones have a wide variety of shapes and sizes to suit their different functions. Many of their shapes are quite complex. The vertebrae, for example, are stacked on top of each other to form the protective channel through which the fragile spinal cord runs. The ossa coxae form the bony pelvis to which the lower limbs attach.

THE SHORT BONES

The short bones are small and more or less cuboidal. Many of their shapes help give joints flexibility; this is the case with the talus, the bone that enables the ankle to turn. The patella, or kneecap, is a short bone whose shape is called "sesamoid" because it resembles the shape of a sesame seed.

The Head

A group of flat, irregular bones

If you look closely at a skull, you will notice that it has fine, irregular lines. These lines are the rigid joints, known as sutures, at the borders of the different cranial bones. The skull, thus, is not a single bone; it is made of eight irregularly shaped bones that gradually fuse together during growth. The numerous bones of the face are also irregular in shape. These bones define the oral cavity, or mouth; the nasal cavities; the orbits, or eye sockets; and the sinuses.

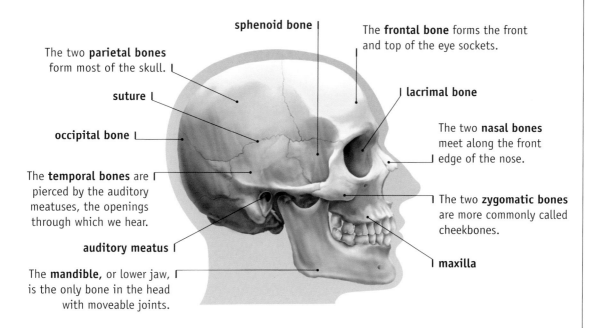

sphenoid bone

The **frontal bone** forms the front and top of the eye sockets.

The two **parietal bones** form most of the skull.

suture

lacrimal bone

occipital bone

The two **nasal bones** meet along the front edge of the nose.

The **temporal bones** are pierced by the auditory meatuses, the openings through which we hear.

The two **zygomatic bones** are more commonly called cheekbones.

auditory meatus

maxilla

The **mandible,** or lower jaw, is the only bone in the head with moveable joints.

INTERIOR OF THE HEAD

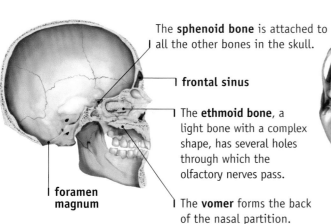

The **sphenoid bone** is attached to all the other bones in the skull.

frontal sinus

The **ethmoid bone**, a light bone with a complex shape, has several holes through which the olfactory nerves pass.

foramen magnum

The **vomer** forms the back of the nasal partition.

BOTTOM OF THE HEAD

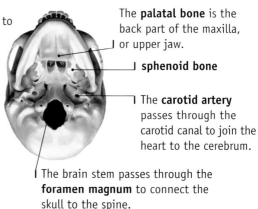

The **palatal bone** is the back part of the maxilla, or upper jaw.

sphenoid bone

The **carotid artery** passes through the carotid canal to join the heart to the cerebrum.

The brain stem passes through the **foramen magnum** to connect the skull to the spine.

THE SKULL OF A NEWBORN

At birth, the bones of the skull are not completely fused together. They are linked by wide membranes called fontanels. These membranes give the skull bones a degree of mobility that enables a child's head to compress during birth and then adapt to the rapid growth of the cerebrum during his or her early years.

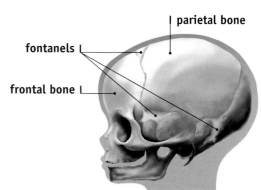

parietal bone

fontanels

frontal bone

The Spine

The spine, also known as the vertebral column, is the central axis of the human body that extends from the back of the skull to the pelvis. It is made of a chain of small bones called vertebrae that house and protect the spinal cord and serve as points of attachment for the ribs and muscles.

THE VERTEBRAE

Human beings have 33 vertebrae. Anatomists divide these bones into five groups: cervical, thoracic, lumbar, sacral, and caudal. Although the different vertebrae have slightly different proportions, all vertebrae have a similar structure; each one has a body from which bony apophyses, or processes, protrude. The column contains a central channel—the spinal foramen—through which the spinal cord passes.

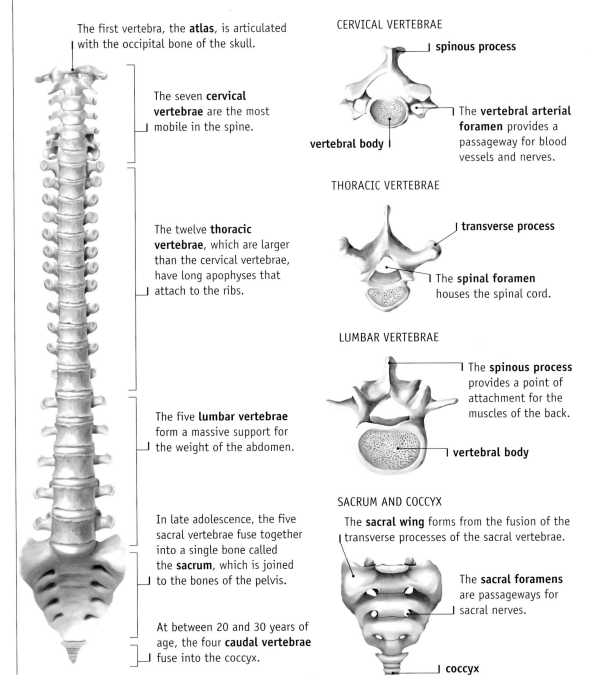

The first vertebra, the **atlas**, is articulated with the occipital bone of the skull.

The seven **cervical vertebrae** are the most mobile in the spine.

The twelve **thoracic vertebrae**, which are larger than the cervical vertebrae, have long apophyses that attach to the ribs.

The five **lumbar vertebrae** form a massive support for the weight of the abdomen.

In late adolescence, the five sacral vertebrae fuse together into a single bone called the **sacrum**, which is joined to the bones of the pelvis.

At between 20 and 30 years of age, the four **caudal vertebrae** fuse into the coccyx.

CERVICAL VERTEBRAE

spinous process

The **vertebral arterial foramen** provides a passageway for blood vessels and nerves.

vertebral body

THORACIC VERTEBRAE

transverse process

The **spinal foramen** houses the spinal cord.

LUMBAR VERTEBRAE

The **spinous process** provides a point of attachment for the muscles of the back.

vertebral body

SACRUM AND COCCYX

The **sacral wing** forms from the fusion of the transverse processes of the sacral vertebrae.

The **sacral foramens** are passageways for sacral nerves.

coccyx

ARTICULATION OF THE VERTEBRAE

Except for those that form the sacrum and the coccyx, all vertebrae are mobile. They are joined to each other with small protrusions called the inferior and superior articular processes. The body of each vertebra rests on an intervertebral disk, a gelatinous mass that acts as a shock absorber. This unique structure makes the spine both strong and very flexible.

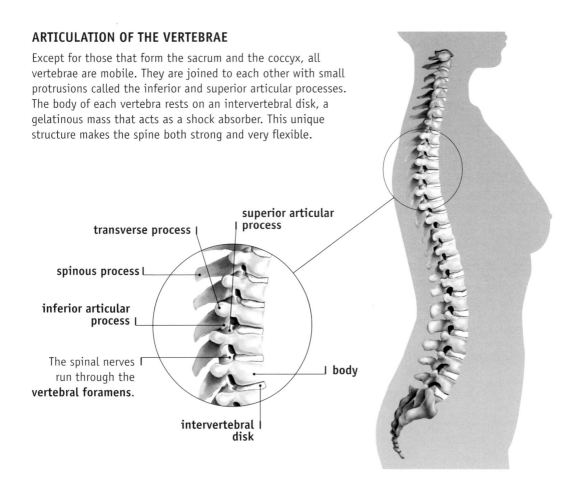

transverse process

superior articular process

spinous process

inferior articular process

The spinal nerves run through the **vertebral foramens.**

body

intervertebral disk

THE RIB CAGE

The thorax, which is the upper part of the human trunk, contains the lungs and the heart. These vital organs are protected by the rib cage, a bony cage formed by 12 pairs of ribs articulated with the thoracic vertebrae and the sternum. The 10 top pairs of ribs are attached to the sternum by costal cartilage, which is flexible enough to allow the rib cage to change shape during breathing. The two lowest pairs of ribs, which are not attached to the sternum, are called floating ribs.

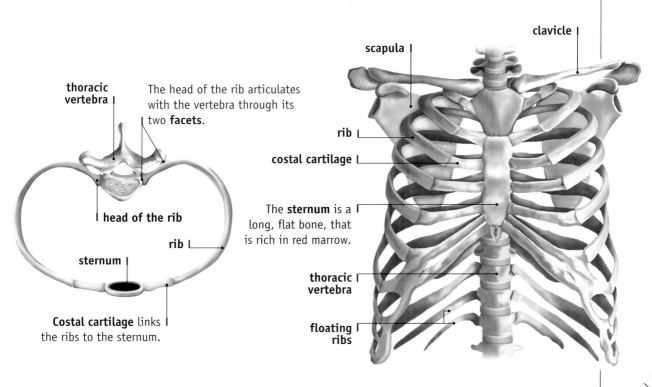

thoracic vertebra

The head of the rib articulates with the vertebra through its two **facets**.

head of the rib

rib

sternum

Costal cartilage links the ribs to the sternum.

scapula

clavicle

rib

costal cartilage

The **sternum** is a long, flat bone, that is rich in red marrow.

thoracic vertebra

floating ribs

The Hands and the Feet

The extremities of the limbs

As the human species has evolved, the functions of the hands and feet have become very differentiated; the hands are used to grasp, while the feet provide stability and mobility for the body. In spite of these functional differences, hands and feet have very similar structures. In both, there are five digits formed of phalanges, a central section composed of five long bones, and a part composed of short bones that joins them to the limb. Our two hands and two feet contain a total of 106 bones—more than half of all the bones in the human skeleton.

THE BONES OF THE HAND

The palm of the hand is formed of five metacarpal bones, each of which is extended by phalanges, the bones that form the fingers. Each finger is composed of proximal, middle, and distal phalanges, except for the thumb, which has only proximal and distal parts. A complex grouping of eight carpal bones makes up the wrist. Two of these—the scaphoid and the lunate—articulate with the radius.

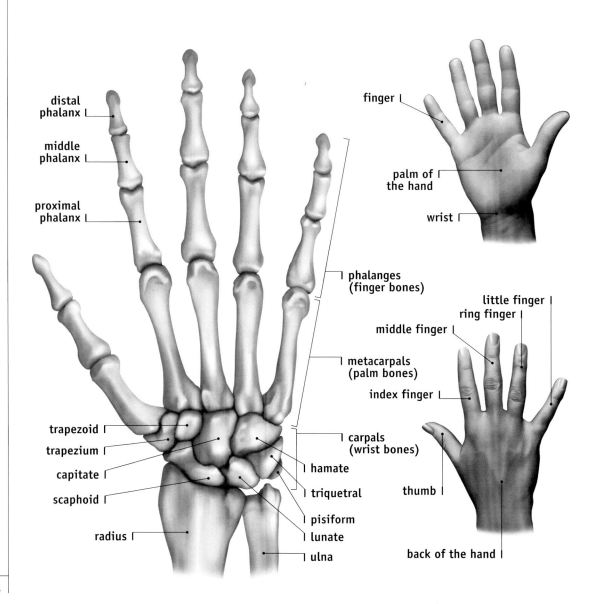

distal phalanx

middle phalanx

proximal phalanx

trapezoid

trapezium

capitate

scaphoid

radius

phalanges (finger bones)

metacarpals (palm bones)

carpals (wrist bones)

hamate

triquetral

pisiform

lunate

ulna

finger

palm of the hand

wrist

little finger

ring finger

middle finger

index finger

thumb

back of the hand

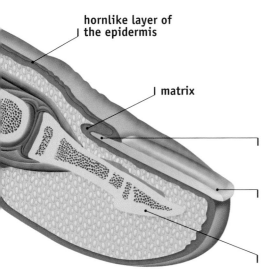

hornlike layer of
the epidermis

matrix

THE NAILS

Each finger and toe has a nail at its end. This small protective plate consists of hornlike epidermal cells produced by a matrix located over the distal phalanx. Nails are hard because of their very high concentration of the protein keratin.

The **base of the nail** is protected by a fold in the skin called the cuticle.

Fingernails grow an average of a tenth of a millimeter every day.

distal phalanx

THE BONES OF THE FOOT

The structure of the foot is similar to that of the hand. The tarsus, a group of seven bones, forms the ankle and articulates with the tibia and fibula. The five bones of the metatarsus, which form the foot itself, extend from the tarsus. The toes consist of phalanges that extend from the metatarsus. Like the fingers, each toe has proximal, middle, and distal phalanges, except for the big toe, which, like the thumb, has just proximal and distal phalanges.

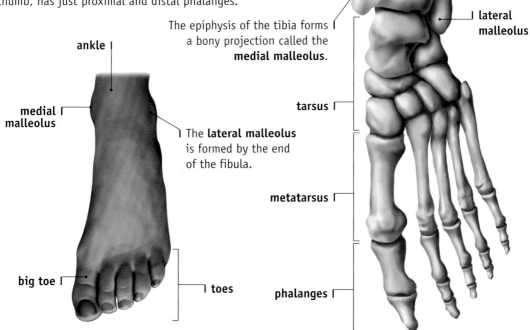

The epiphysis of the tibia forms a bony projection called the **medial malleolus**.

ankle

medial
malleolus

The **lateral malleolus** is formed by the end of the fibula.

big toe

toes

tibia

fibula

lateral
malleolus

tarsus

metatarsus

phalanges

The **talus** is the central bone of the ankle. Tucked behind the ends of the tibia and fibula, it distributes the body's weight between the calcaneus and the navicular bone.

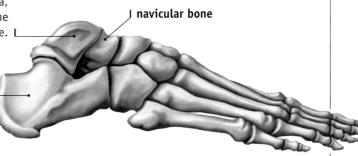

navicular bone

The **calcaneus**, or heel bone, supports much of the body's weight. It is also where the Achilles' tendon attaches the calf muscles to the foot.

The Joints

The junctions between the bones

The points of contact between bones, called joints, are essential for the mobility and solidity of the skeleton. The kind of tissue that forms the joint between two or more bones determines, in large part, the range of movement associated with that joint. Fibrous and cartilaginous joints have very little mobility, while synovial joints allow a wide variety of movements. The nature of the movement allowed by a joint, however, also depends very much on the shapes of the bones it connects.

FIBROUS AND CARTILAGINOUS JOINTS

Certain bones, like those of the skull, are connected by very dense fibrous tissue. These fibrous joints, also called sutures, make bones immobile so that they can perform a protective function.

When two bones are linked by cartilaginous tissue, the joint permits very limited movement. This is the case with the joint between the first rib and the sternum, called the synchondrosis, and the joints between the bones of the pubis, known as symphyses.

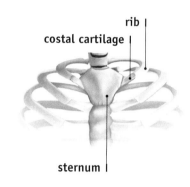

rib |

costal cartilage |

sternum |

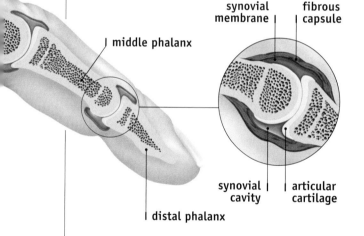

| middle phalanx

synovial membrane |

fibrous capsule |

synovial cavity |

articular cartilage |

| distal phalanx

SYNOVIAL JOINTS

Most joints are mobile—they allow bones to move in relation to other bones, in some cases with great range. Known as synovial joints, these joints are contained in a fibrous capsule that is solidly attached to the periostea of the bones they connect. The membrane that lines the interior of the capsule produces **synovial fluid**, which fills the area around the joint, called the synovial cavity. This fluid lubricates the joint and nourishes the cartilage that covers the ends of the bones.

LIGAMENTS

Most bones are connected to each other by fibrous tissues, called ligaments, that stabilize and reinforce synovial joints. The knee joint alone has several types of ligaments. On both sides of the leg, collateral ligaments join the femur to the tibia and fibula and prevent the knee from moving from side to side. The patellar ligament strengthens the joint from the front, while the cruciate ligaments restrict the knee from moving front to back.

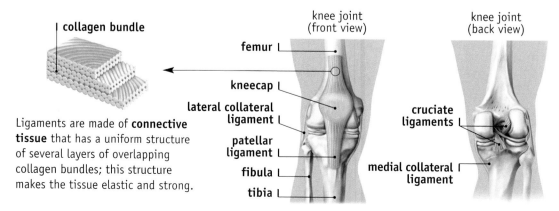

| collagen bundle

Ligaments are made of **connective tissue** that has a uniform structure of several layers of overlapping collagen bundles; this structure makes the tissue elastic and strong.

knee joint (front view)

femur |
kneecap |
lateral collateral ligament |
patellar ligament |
fibula |
tibia |

knee joint (back view)

cruciate ligaments |

medial collateral ligament |

DIFFERENT TYPES OF SYNOVIAL JOINTS

Synovial joints are divided into six categories. They permit a wide variety of movements, including gliding, hinging, pivoting, two-way rotation, and circular, or three-way, rotation.

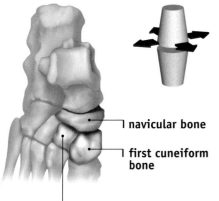

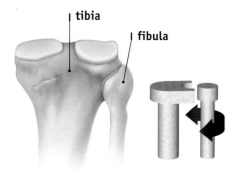

navicular bone

first cuneiform bone

second cuneiform bone

Gliding joints permit only small lateral movements. They are found between the vertebrae and the ribs, in the carpus (wrist joint) and the tarsus (ankle joint), and between the navicular bone and the cuneiform bones.

The elbow is a **hinge joint** that allows flexion and extension along a single axis. The convex projection of the humerus moves back and forth within the hollow of the ulna.

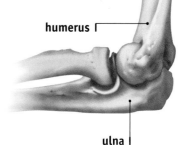

humerus

ulna

tibia

fibula

A **pivot joint** allows a bone whose end fits into a ring of bone or ligament to turn on its longitudinal axis.

lunate bone

radius bone

scaphoid bone

An **ellipsoidal joint**, also called a condyloid joint, is described as biaxial because it allows movement on two different axes. The wrist joint, in which the scaphoid and lunate bones turn in the cavity of the radius, is an ellipsoidal joint.

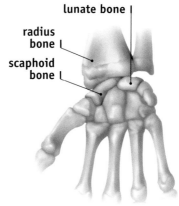

humerus

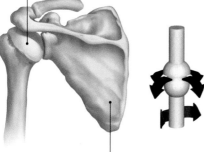

The hip and shoulder joints are **ball joints**. These joints allow movements along three axes; by turning in the glenoid cavity of the scapula, the humerus can move in a complete circle.

shoulder blade

A **saddle joint** resembles an ellipsoidal joint, but, because its bony ends have convex and concave surfaces, this kind of joint allows movements of even greater range. The joint between the metacarpal bone of the thumb and the trapezium of the wrist is a good example of a saddle joint.

trapezium

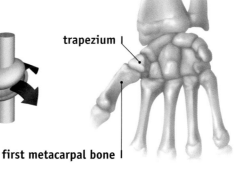

first metacarpal bone

The Skeletal Muscles

Motion generators

There are muscles in every part of the human body—everywhere from the face to the limbs to the viscera. Numbering more than 600 in all, they represent almost half of our body mass. Most of our muscles are attached to the bones of the skeleton and are, thus, known as skeletal muscles. Skeletal muscles contract, pulling their ends closer together, when they receive messages in the form of nerve impulses; these contractions cause bones to move in their joints. Skeletal muscles are also responsible for maintaining body posture.

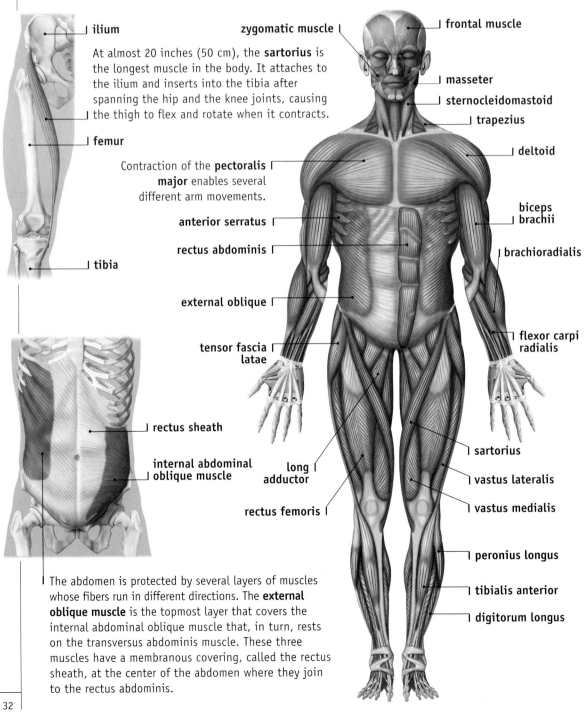

ilium

At almost 20 inches (50 cm), the **sartorius** is the longest muscle in the body. It attaches to the ilium and inserts into the tibia after spanning the hip and the knee joints, causing the thigh to flex and rotate when it contracts.

femur

Contraction of the **pectoralis major** enables several different arm movements.

anterior serratus

rectus abdominis

tibia

external oblique

tensor fascia latae

rectus sheath

internal abdominal oblique muscle

long adductor

rectus femoris

zygomatic muscle

frontal muscle

masseter

sternocleidomastoid

trapezius

deltoid

biceps brachii

brachioradialis

flexor carpi radialis

sartorius

vastus lateralis

vastus medialis

peronius longus

tibialis anterior

digitorum longus

The abdomen is protected by several layers of muscles whose fibers run in different directions. The **external oblique muscle** is the topmost layer that covers the internal abdominal oblique muscle that, in turn, rests on the transversus abdominis muscle. These three muscles have a membranous covering, called the rectus sheath, at the center of the abdomen where they join to the rectus abdominis.

TENDONS: BETWEEN MUSCLES AND BONES

Skeletal muscles span one or more joints and attach to bones by whitish, fibrous bundles called tendons. Contraction of a muscle generally makes only one bone move, while the other stays immobile. The point at which the muscle is attached to the immobile bone is called the origin of the muscle, while the place where the muscle meets the mobile bone is called the insertion.

The central fleshy part of the muscle is called the belly. Some muscles have several origins and, therefore, several bellies. Depending on the number of tendons they have, these muscles are called biceps, triceps, or quadriceps.

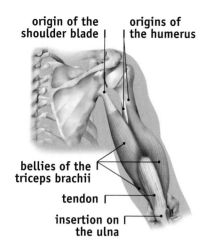

origin of the shoulder blade

origins of the humerus

bellies of the triceps brachii

tendon

insertion on the ulna

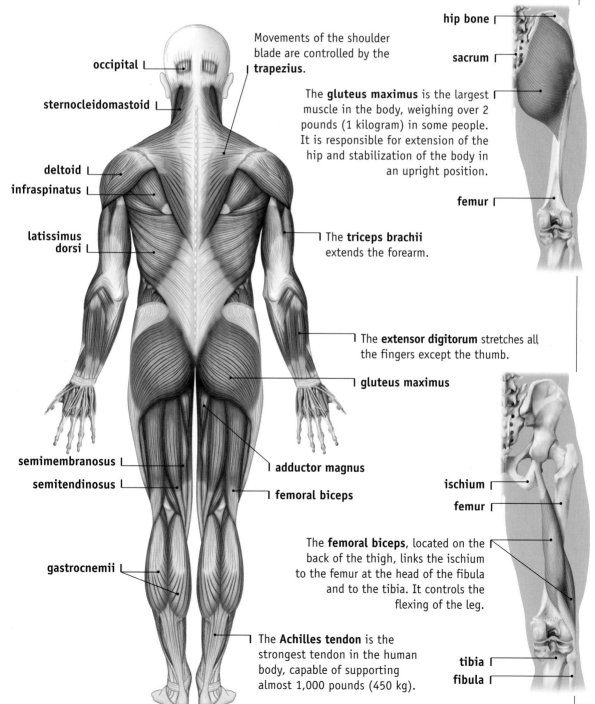

occipital

sternocleidomastoid

deltoid

infraspinatus

latissimus dorsi

semimembranosus

semitendinosus

gastrocnemii

Movements of the shoulder blade are controlled by the **trapezius**.

The **gluteus maximus** is the largest muscle in the body, weighing over 2 pounds (1 kilogram) in some people. It is responsible for extension of the hip and stabilization of the body in an upright position.

The **triceps brachii** extends the forearm.

The **extensor digitorum** stretches all the fingers except the thumb.

gluteus maximus

adductor magnus

femoral biceps

The **femoral biceps**, located on the back of the thigh, links the ischium to the femur at the head of the fibula and to the tibia. It controls the flexing of the leg.

The **Achilles tendon** is the strongest tendon in the human body, capable of supporting almost 1,000 pounds (450 kg).

hip bone

sacrum

femur

ischium

femur

tibia

fibula

Muscle Tissue

Bundles of contractile cells

When fibers that make up skeletal muscles are examined under a microscope, long filaments can be seen within muscle cells. These filaments, called myofibrils, have very specific colored striations, or alternating dark and light bands, that are intimately connected to the mechanism that causes contraction of the muscle fibers.

THE ANATOMY OF SKELETAL MUSCLES

The skeletal muscles are composed mainly of filiform muscle fibers that have an average length of about 1 inch (3 cm) but can be up to 20 inches (50 cm) long. Grouped in highly vascularized bundles, these cells contain long threads called myofibrils.

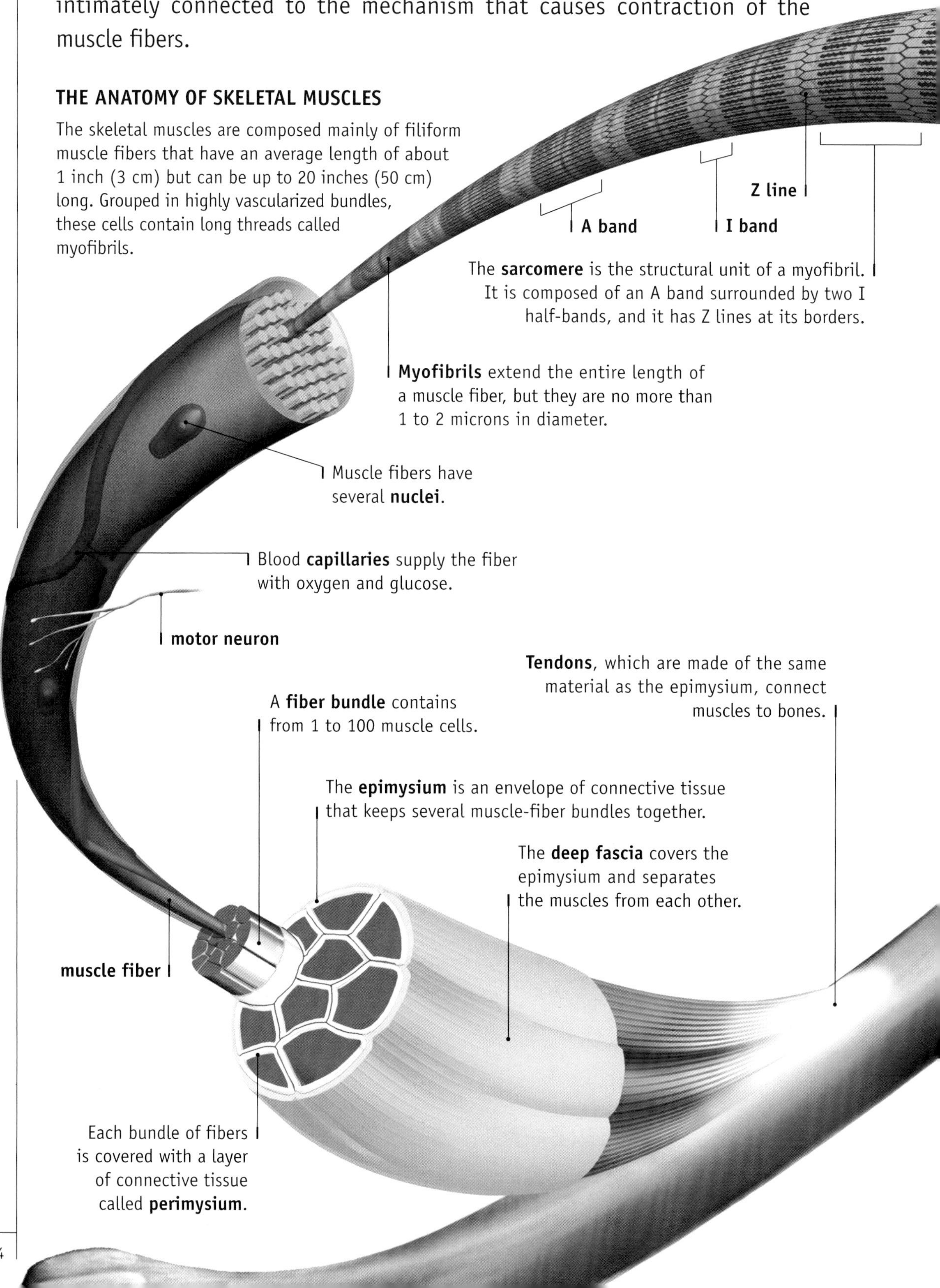

A band

Z line

I band

The **sarcomere** is the structural unit of a myofibril. It is composed of an A band surrounded by two I half-bands, and it has Z lines at its borders.

Myofibrils extend the entire length of a muscle fiber, but they are no more than 1 to 2 microns in diameter.

Muscle fibers have several **nuclei**.

Blood **capillaries** supply the fiber with oxygen and glucose.

motor neuron

Tendons, which are made of the same material as the epimysium, connect muscles to bones.

A **fiber bundle** contains from 1 to 100 muscle cells.

The **epimysium** is an envelope of connective tissue that keeps several muscle-fiber bundles together.

The **deep fascia** covers the epimysium and separates the muscles from each other.

muscle fiber

Each bundle of fibers is covered with a layer of connective tissue called **perimysium**.

THICK AND THIN FILAMENTS

The characteristic bands that appear along myofibrils are caused by the thick and thin filaments of which they are made. The darker-colored A bands are composed of both thick and thin filaments, while the lighter-colored I bands contain only thin filaments.

Myosin is the main component of thick filaments. The molecules of this protein, which are arranged in bundles, face outward. The thin filaments are composed of the proteins actin, tropomyosin, and troponin.

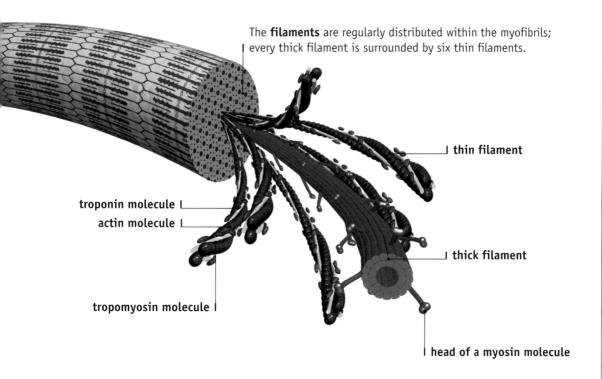

The **filaments** are regularly distributed within the myofibrils; every thick filament is surrounded by six thin filaments.

thin filament

troponin molecule

actin molecule

thick filament

tropomyosin molecule

head of a myosin molecule

CONTRACTION OF SKELETAL MUSCLES

In a muscle at rest ❶, the thick and thin filaments of the muscle's myofibrils are loosely interlaced in such a way that the spaces between two consecutive thick filaments form I bands.

When a neuron transmits a nerve impulse to a muscle fiber ❷, the heads of the myosin molecules in the thick filaments are energized. They connect with the actin molecules of the thin filaments, where they discharge their energy. This reaction makes the thin filament slide toward the center of the A band, which shortens the sarcomeres. As the sarcomeres shorten, the muscle fiber contracts.

When the nerve impulse stops, a chemical reaction blocks interaction between the myosin and actin molecules, and the thin filaments return to their initial positions. This reaction causes the muscle fiber to relax.

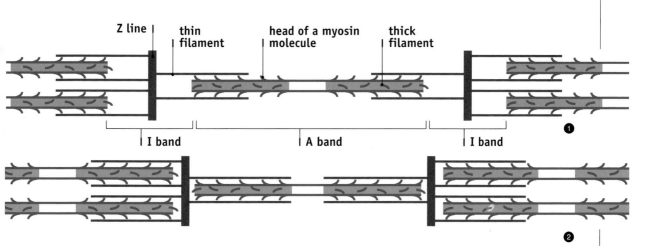

Z line

thin filament

head of a myosin molecule

thick filament

I band

A band

I band

❶

❷

The Muscles of the Head

An infinite variety of movements

The movements of the human face are numerous and extremely varied. Smiling, blinking, chewing, frowning, and pouting are only a few of them. No fewer than 50 muscles, some of them very small, are always at work under the skin of a human head, enabling us to eat, speak, see, nod, and express emotions. Facial expressions are a mode of communication in themselves.

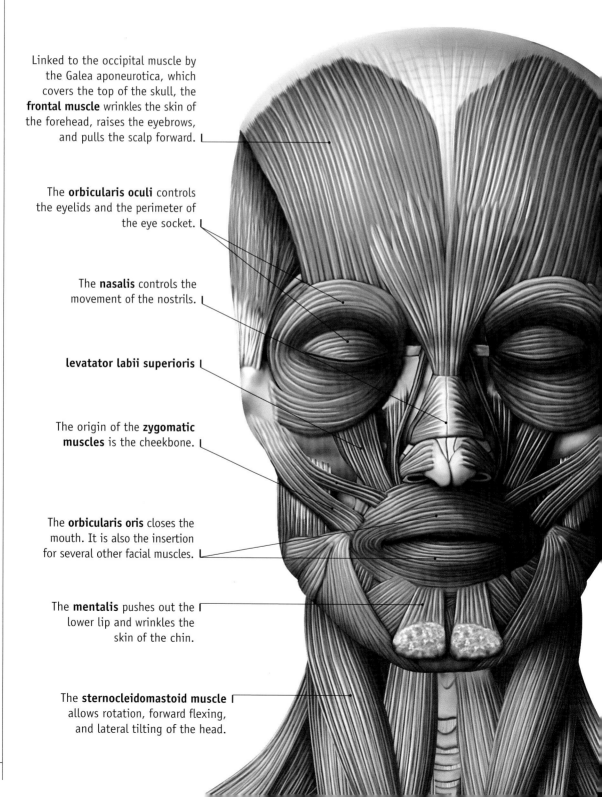

Linked to the occipital muscle by the Galea aponeurotica, which covers the top of the skull, the **frontal muscle** wrinkles the skin of the forehead, raises the eyebrows, and pulls the scalp forward.

The **orbicularis oculi** controls the eyelids and the perimeter of the eye socket.

The **nasalis** controls the movement of the nostrils.

levatator labii superioris

The origin of the **zygomatic muscles** is the cheekbone.

The **orbicularis oris** closes the mouth. It is also the insertion for several other facial muscles.

The **mentalis** pushes out the lower lip and wrinkles the skin of the chin.

The **sternocleidomastoid muscle** allows rotation, forward flexing, and lateral tilting of the head.

FACIAL EXPRESSIONS

Although they are not very powerful, the facial muscles are capable of controlling the small movements of the skin that change the appearance of the human face, causing a wide variety of expressions. Some facial expressions have universally recognized and understood meanings—showing, for example, joy, anger, or surprise—while others are more subtle and personal.

zygomatics

triangularis

corrugator

frontal

orbicularis of the mouth

MUSCLES UNDER THE SKIN

Most of the muscles in the head are unusual in that they do not control the movement of a bone but act on the skin of the face. This is why they are called skin muscles, also known as mimic muscles. The orbicularis muscles of the eye and the mouth are particularly important skin muscles. They are sphincters, or ring-shaped muscles, that cause orifices to open or close. On the other hand, the masseter and temporal muscles are not skin muscles but mastication muscles. Inserted on the mandible, they control the closing of the jaw.

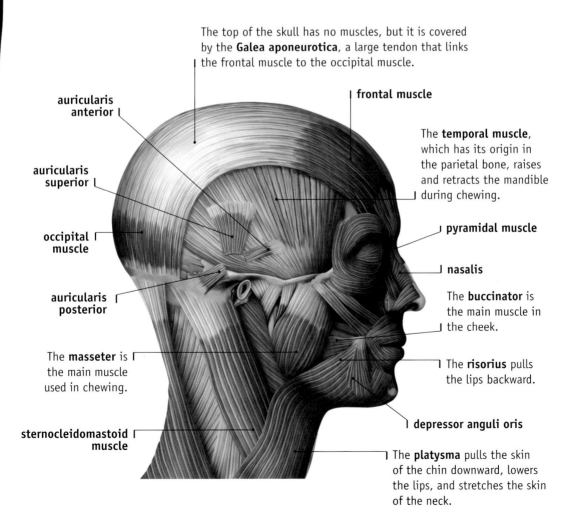

The top of the skull has no muscles, but it is covered by the **Galea aponeurotica**, a large tendon that links the frontal muscle to the occipital muscle.

frontal muscle

The **temporal muscle**, which has its origin in the parietal bone, raises and retracts the mandible during chewing.

pyramidal muscle

nasalis

The **buccinator** is the main muscle in the cheek.

The **risorius** pulls the lips backward.

depressor anguli oris

The **platysma** pulls the skin of the chin downward, lowers the lips, and stretches the skin of the neck.

auricularis anterior

auricularis superior

occipital muscle

auricularis posterior

The **masseter** is the main muscle used in chewing.

sternocleidomastoid muscle

The Action of the Skeletal Muscles

From contraction to movement

Unlike the involuntary actions of the smooth and cardiac muscles, the movements controlled by the skeletal muscles are voluntary—we decide to walk, talk, or pick up an object. Most movements that we make, however, involve a number of muscles acting together without us being completely aware of them. In fact, a single muscle cannot function in isolation, since it is capable of only one action: contraction.

AGONIST AND ANTAGONIST MUSCLES

Most movements of the skeletal bones are caused by opposing pairs of muscles located on opposite sides of a joint. The muscle that contracts first in a movement is called the agonist, while the opposed muscle, which resists the movement, is called the antagonist. For the movement to be reversed, the muscles must switch roles. This is what happens with the two main muscles of the upper arm—the biceps, located at the front, and the triceps, at the back—as the arm bends and straightens.

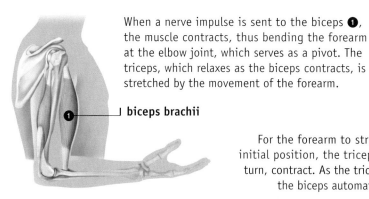

When a nerve impulse is sent to the biceps ❶, the muscle contracts, thus bending the forearm at the elbow joint, which serves as a pivot. The triceps, which relaxes as the biceps contracts, is stretched by the movement of the forearm.

biceps brachii

triceps brachii

For the forearm to straighten to its initial position, the triceps ❷ must, in turn, contract. As the triceps contracts, the biceps automatically relaxes.

THE EYE MUSCLES

Humans can orient their eyeballs very quickly and accurately toward the objects that they want to look at. This ability is provided by the six skeletal muscles that connect each eye to its eye socket. Through the coordinated action of these muscles, we can turn our eyes along three axes.

The **trochlea** is a fibrocartilaginous pulley through which the tendon of the superior oblique muscle passes.

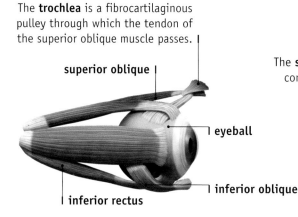

superior oblique

eyeball

inferior rectus

inferior oblique

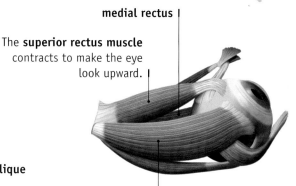

medial rectus

The **superior rectus muscle** contracts to make the eye look upward.

lateral rectus

The Movements of the Hand

Incredible dexterity

Human beings can grasp and manipulate objects with great precision. This ability is unique in the animal kingdom. Our dexterity is due to the skeletal structure of the human hand and the complex group of muscles in the forearm. These features enable us to make movements as varied as playing the piano, turning a water faucet, and writing a letter.

THE ANTERIOR MUSCLES OF THE HAND AND FOREARM

The muscles responsible for flexion of the wrist, hand, and fingers are located on the anterior face of the forearm. Most of them originate at the end of the humerus just above the elbow and connect to the metacarpal bones and phalanges with long tendons. Several ligaments and a membrane called the palmar aponeurosis protect these tendons. The hand also contains a number of intrinsic muscles, including the one that provides the thumb with mobility.

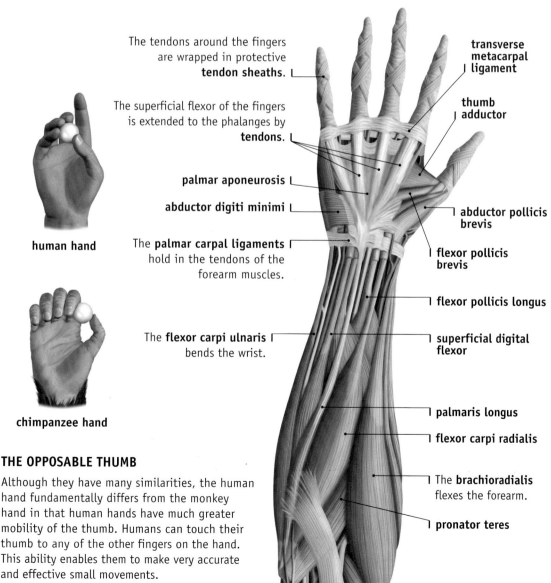

The tendons around the fingers are wrapped in protective **tendon sheaths.**

The superficial flexor of the fingers is extended to the phalanges by **tendons.**

palmar aponeurosis

abductor digiti minimi

The **palmar carpal ligaments** hold in the tendons of the forearm muscles.

The **flexor carpi ulnaris** bends the wrist.

human hand

chimpanzee hand

transverse metacarpal ligament

thumb adductor

abductor pollicis brevis

flexor pollicis brevis

flexor pollicis longus

superficial digital flexor

palmaris longus

flexor carpi radialis

The **brachioradialis** flexes the forearm.

pronator teres

THE OPPOSABLE THUMB

Although they have many similarities, the human hand fundamentally differs from the monkey hand in that human hands have much greater mobility of the thumb. Humans can touch their thumb to any of the other fingers on the hand. This ability enables them to make very accurate and effective small movements.

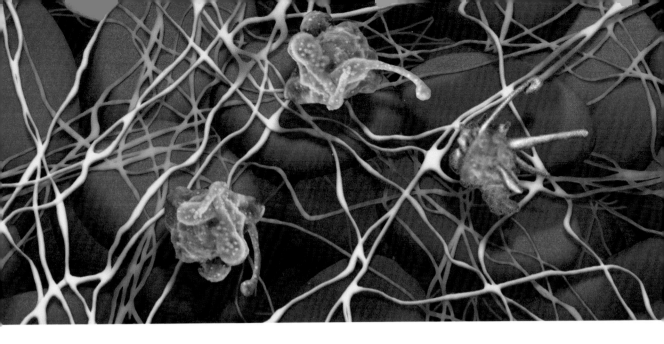

Blood, propelled by regular contractions of the cardiac muscle, plays a number of very important roles in the human body. As it flows through the vast network of veins, arteries, and capillaries, blood carries oxygen and nutrients that are indispensable to cells, and it removes waste materials such as carbon dioxide. It also carries hormones and white blood cells to most parts of the body.

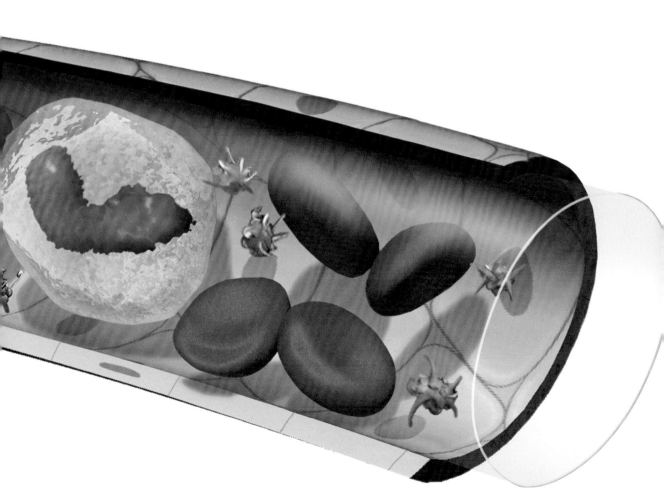

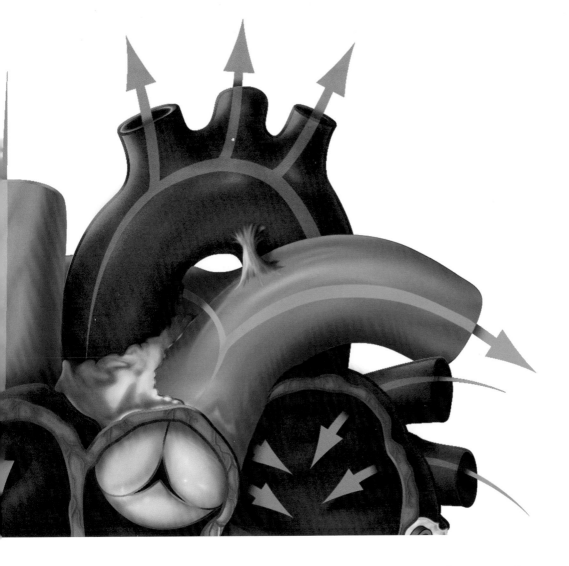

Blood Circulation

Blood

A means of transport and defense

Blood, which contributes 8 percent of our body weight, moves through a vast, closed network of arteries and veins. It infuses all the tissues of the body, providing them with oxygen and nutritive substances and removing their waste. Blood also carries white blood cells and hormones throughout the body.

THE COMPOSITION OF BLOOD

Blood consists of cells and cell fragments floating in a watery, yellowish liquid called plasma. There are two main types of blood cells: red blood cells, or erythrocytes, and white blood cells, or leucocytes. Compared to the number of red blood cells, there are relatively few white blood cells. Despite this, there are many types of white blood cells, including neutrophils, lymphocytes, monocytes, eosinophils, and basophils. Finally, blood contains platelets, which are not true cells but fragments of giant cells.

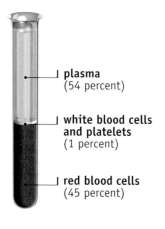

plasma
(54 percent)

white blood cells and platelets
(1 percent)

red blood cells
(45 percent)

blood vessel

Blood **plasma** is 90 percent water. Beside water, it also consists of proteins, vitamins, and other solutes.

Monocytes are the largest white blood cells. Blood carries them to the other tissues, to which they adhere.

Blood platelets, or thrombocytes, are fragments of giant blood cells found in bone marrow called megacaryocytes. These large cells have life spans of only 5 to 10 days, and they are involved in blood coagulation.

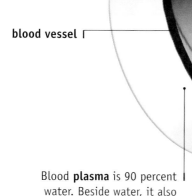

COAGULATION

When a blood vessel is damaged, several mechanisms combine to stop the hemorrhage. First, platelets stick to each other and plug small holes in the blood vessel. Then the plasma produces a filamentous protein, called fibrin, which forms a net that holds red blood cells together to make a scab.

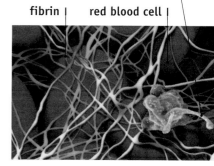

platelet

fibrin   **red blood cell**

THE FORMATION OF BLOOD CELLS

Red blood cells, platelets, and white blood cells such as neutrophils all come from hemocytoblasts, which are cells produced by red bone marrow. Lymphocytes and monocytes also originate from hemocytoblasts, but they complete their differentiation in the lymphoid tissues.

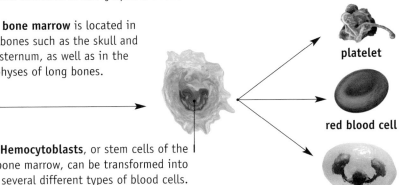

Red bone marrow is located in flat bones such as the skull and the sternum, as well as in the epiphyses of long bones.

Hemocytoblasts, or stem cells of the bone marrow, can be transformed into several different types of blood cells.

platelet

red blood cell

neutrophil

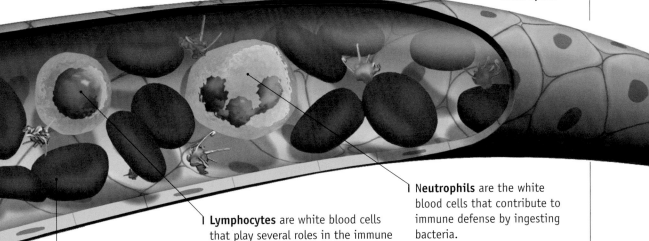

red blood cell

Lymphocytes are white blood cells that play several roles in the immune system, but there are relatively few of them in the blood.

Neutrophils are the white blood cells that contribute to immune defense by ingesting bacteria.

A heme includes an **oxygen** molecule and an iron ion.

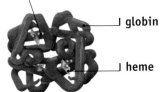

globin

heme

hemoglobin molecule

RED BLOOD CELLS

Our bodies contain an average of 25 billion red blood cells, or erythrocytes. These cells have no nuclei, and they are capable of stretching and deforming in order to pass through the narrowest blood vessels. Each red blood cell contains about 250 million molecules of hemoglobin, a substance formed of the protein globin and four pigments called hemes. Hemoglobin plays an essential role in gas exchange by transporting oxygen and carbon dioxide through the blood. Blood gets its red color when the iron in the hemes combines with oxygen.

BLOOD TYPES

Red blood cells carry antigens, or substances that can be attacked by antibodies, on their surfaces. Among the 100 known antigens, two are used to determine the different blood types. Types A and B respectively designate the carriers of antigens A and B. Type AB designates carriers of both antigens. Finally, type O refers to those that carry neither antigen A nor antigen B.

Blood plasma contains antibodies that react to antigens that are normally absent from our blood. Therefore, in a blood transfusion, it is essential that the blood types of the donor and the receiver are compatible. If the donated blood contains an unwelcome antigen, the receiver's body will reject the transfusion.

COMPATIBILITY OF
BLOOD GROUPS

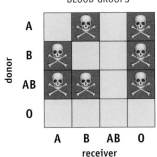

donor

receiver

The Cardiovascular System

Two blood circuits

The blood, the heart, and the blood vessels constitute the circulatory, or cardiovascular, system. Continually propelled by the heart, blood flows through the body in two distinct circuits: the pulmonary and systemic bloodstreams. All the blood in the body flows through the heart once per minute.

A HUGE CLOSED-CIRCUIT NETWORK

The blood vessels in the human body form a vast network with a total length of around 93,000 miles (150,000 kilometers). The heart pumps blood out through arteries, or vessels leading from the heart, and receives blood back through veins, or vessels leading to the heart. Arteries and veins branch into smaller vessels called arterioles and venules, which, in turn, branch further into tiny channels called capillaries.

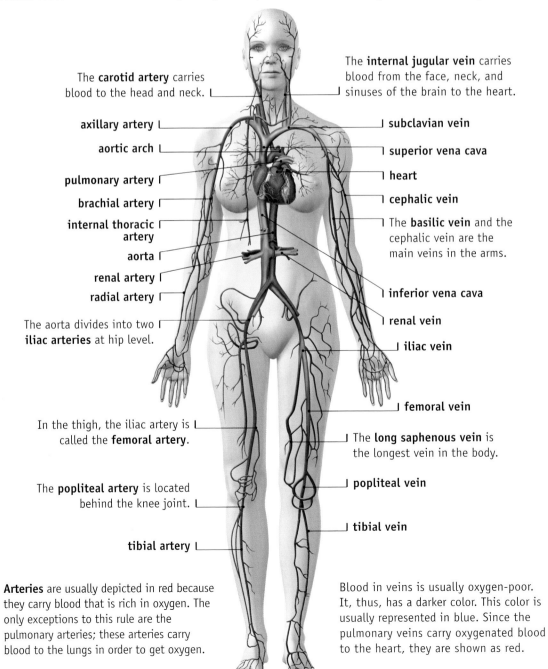

The **carotid artery** carries blood to the head and neck.

The **internal jugular vein** carries blood from the face, neck, and sinuses of the brain to the heart.

axillary artery

aortic arch

pulmonary artery

brachial artery

internal thoracic artery

aorta

renal artery

radial artery

The aorta divides into two **iliac arteries** at hip level.

In the thigh, the iliac artery is called the **femoral artery**.

The **popliteal artery** is located behind the knee joint.

tibial artery

subclavian vein

superior vena cava

heart

cephalic vein

The **basilic vein** and the cephalic vein are the main veins in the arms.

inferior vena cava

renal vein

iliac vein

femoral vein

The **long saphenous vein** is the longest vein in the body.

popliteal vein

tibial vein

Arteries are usually depicted in red because they carry blood that is rich in oxygen. The only exceptions to this rule are the pulmonary arteries; these arteries carry blood to the lungs in order to get oxygen.

Blood in veins is usually oxygen-poor. It, thus, has a darker color. This color is usually represented in blue. Since the pulmonary veins carry oxygenated blood to the heart, they are shown as red.

THE TWO CARDIOVASCULAR CIRCUITS

The pulmonary bloodstream includes the pulmonary arteries, veins, and capillaries. The right ventricle of the heart pumps blood through the pulmonary arteries to the lungs, where it is oxygenated and the carbon dioxide in it is removed. The pulmonary veins return this oxygenated blood to the heart, where it is pumped out into the systemic bloodstream.

The systemic bloodstream is composed of all the other blood vessels in the body. Its blood is expelled from the left ventricle through the aorta; it circulates through all body tissues except the lungs.

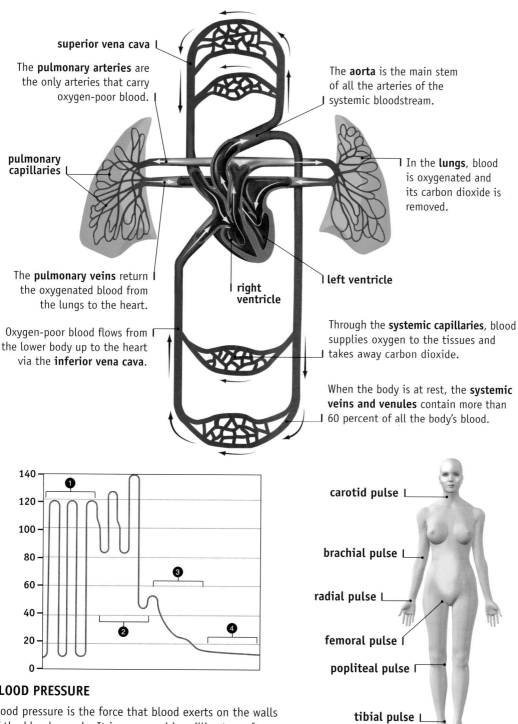

superior vena cava

The **pulmonary arteries** are the only arteries that carry oxygen-poor blood.

The **aorta** is the main stem of all the arteries of the systemic bloodstream.

pulmonary capillaries

In the **lungs**, blood is oxygenated and its carbon dioxide is removed.

The **pulmonary veins** return the oxygenated blood from the lungs to the heart.

right ventricle

left ventricle

Oxygen-poor blood flows from the lower body up to the heart via the **inferior vena cava**.

Through the **systemic capillaries**, blood supplies oxygen to the tissues and takes away carbon dioxide.

When the body is at rest, the **systemic veins and venules** contain more than 60 percent of all the body's blood.

carotid pulse

brachial pulse

radial pulse

femoral pulse

popliteal pulse

tibial pulse

BLOOD PRESSURE

Blood pressure is the force that blood exerts on the walls of the blood vessels. It is measured in millimeters of mercury. Blood pressure is irregular in the heart ❶ and very high in the arteries ❷. It diminishes considerably when blood reaches the capillaries ❸, and it falls even lower when blood enters the veins ❹.

Each time blood is expelled from the heart, it creates a wave, called the **pulse**, that is perceptible in certain arteries that are close to the skin's surface. One's pulse rate increases as one's physical exertion increases.

45

Arteries and Veins

A closed circuit for irrigation

Blood circulates throughout the whole human body except for certain very localized areas, such as the enamel of the teeth and the cornea of the eye. It moves through two types of blood vessels—arteries and veins—that are distinguished from each other by their structure and by their specialized roles in the cardiovascular system.

THE ANATOMY OF BLOOD VESSELS

The walls of blood vessels, which must resist variations in blood pressure, are composed of three concentric layers of tissue called tunicas. The tunica intima, or inside layer, which is composed of endothelium and a basement membrane, defines the channel within which blood circulates, called the lumen. The tunica intima is covered by a layer of smooth muscle and elastic fibers that form the tunica media, or middle layer. The tunica adventita, or outside layer, is made mainly of collagen fibers.

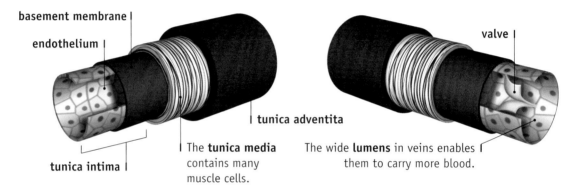

basement membrane

endothelium

valve

tunica adventita

tunica intima

The **tunica media** contains many muscle cells.

The wide **lumens** in veins enables them to carry more blood.

The thickness of the smooth muscle in **arteries** enables them to contract to maintain arterial tension and facilitate circulation of blood from the heart.

Veins have thinner middle layers and wider lumens than arteries. Some veins in the lower limbs have valves that keep blood from flowing downward when a person is standing upright.

THE CAPILLARIES

Capillaries, which consist of a thin layer of endothelial cells covered by a basement membrane, are very small blood vessels; they measure only .01 to .04 inch (.3 to 1 mm) in length and have a maximum diameter of .0004 inch (.01 mm). The extreme thinness of capillary walls allows exchanges between the blood and the space around these tiny vessels. Through the capillaries, oxygen and nutrients are distributed to the tissues, and carbon dioxide, the byproduct of cellular metabolic activity, is carried away.

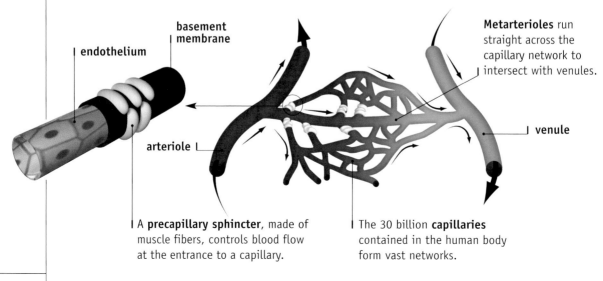

basement membrane

endothelium

Metarterioles run straight across the capillary network to intersect with venules.

arteriole

venule

A **precapillary sphincter**, made of muscle fibers, controls blood flow at the entrance to a capillary.

The 30 billion **capillaries** contained in the human body form vast networks.

CAPILLARY CIRCULATION

Blood flow in the capillary networks is based on the tissues' need for oxygen. A muscle at rest requires less blood than an active muscle. The precapillary sphincters control blood flow in the capillaries through a process of contracting and relaxing.

When a muscle is at rest ❶, a series of sphincters contracts, cutting blood flow in the capillaries.

When the precapillary sphincters are relaxed, blood is free to irrigate the capillary networks of an active muscle ❷.

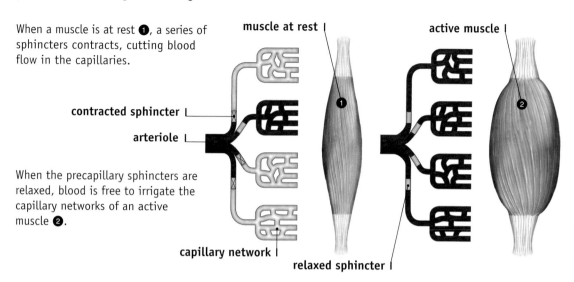

muscle at rest

active muscle

contracted sphincter

arteriole

capillary network

relaxed sphincter

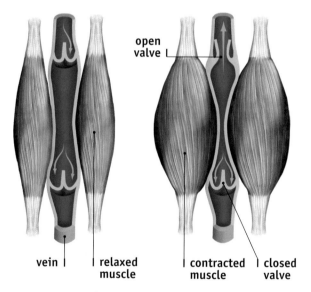

open valve

vein

relaxed muscle

contracted muscle

closed valve

BLOOD CIRCULATION IN THE VEINS

Blood pools in veins in the lower limbs because the force of gravity creates pressure that distends the elastic walls of the veins. Skeletal muscles that lie near the veins facilitate blood circulation from the lower extremities by contracting. These muscle contractions compress the walls of the veins and force the valves located above them to open and let blood flow toward the heart. Since they can open only in one direction, the valves located below the muscles keep the blood from descending. This mechanism is known both as the venous pump and as the muscular pump.

THE SPEED OF BLOOD FLOW

Blood flows more slowly in capillaries than in larger vessels. This slowing makes it possible for exchanges to occur between the blood and the tissues.

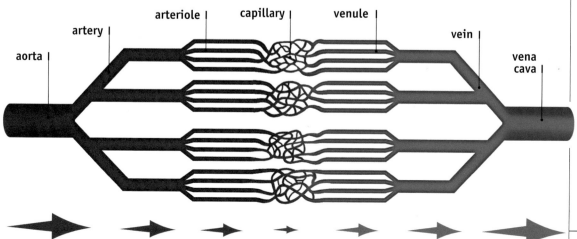

aorta

artery

arteriole

capillary

venule

vein

vena cava

The Heart

A tireless pump

In spite of its small size, the heart is the most active organ in the body. Its muscle fibers contract at an average rate of 70 contractions per minute, rhythmically propelling blood through the body over an entire lifetime. With its complex system of chambers and valves, the heart is a formidable dynamo that pumps 2.6 million quarts (2.5 million liters) of blood each year.

EXTERNAL SURFACE OF THE HEART

The heart is a small organ—measuring only 4 to 5 inches (10 to 12 centimeters) in diameter and weighing an average of only 10.5 ounces (300 grams)—located in the rib cage, between the lungs. Its surface is divided by clefts along which run the coronary arteries and veins that are responsible for blood perfusion of the cardiac muscle. These clefts mark the boundaries between the atria and the ventricles.

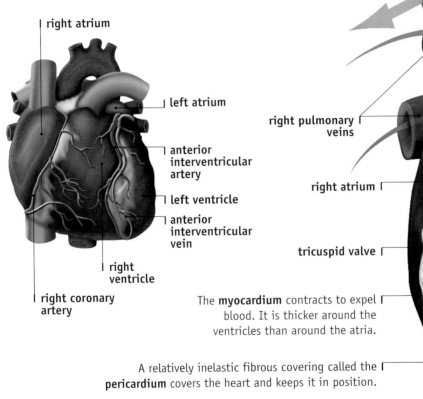

right atrium

left atrium

anterior interventricular artery

left ventricle

anterior interventricular vein

right ventricle

right coronary artery

superior vena cava

right pulmonary artery

right pulmonary veins

right atrium

tricuspid valve

The **myocardium** contracts to expel blood. It is thicker around the ventricles than around the atria.

A relatively inelastic fibrous covering called the **pericardium** covers the heart and keeps it in position.

Pericardial fluid is a lubricant that reduces the friction caused by cardiac pulses.

endocardium

epicardium

inferior vena cava

THE CARDIAC MUSCLE

The heart is composed mostly of the myocardium, or cardiac muscle, which makes up a thick wall of striated muscle fibers. The interior surface of the myocardium, known as the endocardium, is lined with a thin layer of cells that are similar to those that cover all blood vessels. The myocardium is covered with the epicardium, a thin membrane that is the inside layer of the pericardium.

The **aorta** is the largest blood vessel in the human body. It is about 1 inch (2.5 cm) in diameter.

FOUR CHAMBERS, FOUR VALVES

The heart has two parts, separated by the septum, that do not communicate directly. Each part has two chambers, an atrium and a ventricle. The **atria** are the chambers that receive blood from the veins; venae cavae flow into the right atrium, while pulmonary veins flow into the left atrium. The larger **ventricles** expel blood into the arteries; the right ventricle pumps blood into the pulmonary trunk, while the left ventricle pumps blood into the aorta.

All four chambers have valves designed to impede backflow of blood when the heart contracts. The **atrioventricular valves**—the tricuspid valve and the mitral valve—are located between the atria and the ventricles. The **semilunar valves**—the pulmonary valve and the aortic valve—are located at the exits from the ventricles.

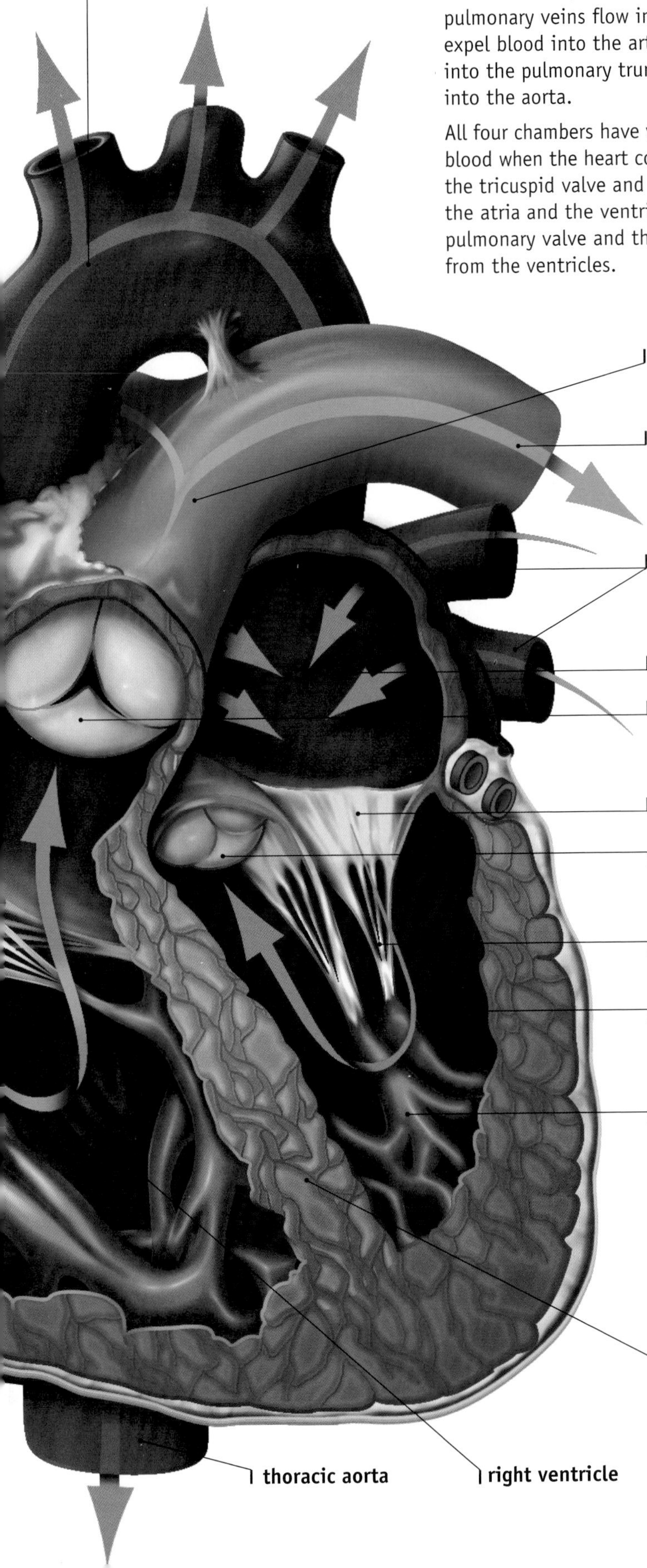

pulmonary trunk

left pulmonary artery

left pulmonary veins

left atrium

pulmonary valve

When the left ventricle contracts, the **mitral valve** is closed by blood pressure.

The **aortic valve** closes after blood is expelled into the aorta.

chordae tendineae

left ventricle

Due to the chordae tendineae, the **papillary muscles** keep the tricuspid and mitral valves from being pushed into the atria when the ventricles contract.

The **intraventricular septum** separates the two ventricles.

thoracic aorta

right ventricle

The Cardiac Cycle

A remarkably regular rhythm

The contractions of the myocardium follow a regular cycle with three distinct phases. Each cycle is triggered by particular cells in the cardiac muscle. These cells are referred to as autorhythmic because they are capable of spontaneously generating and propagating electrical impulses. Since proper functioning of the cardiovascular system depends on the regularity and coordination of the heart's movements, autorhythmic cardiac stimulators are essential.

THE CARDIAC CYCLE

It takes about .8 second for a little more than 2 ounces (70 milliliters) of blood to enter the heart, pass through it, and be expelled into the arteries. This cycle includes a rest phase, called diastole, and two contraction phases, called systoles.

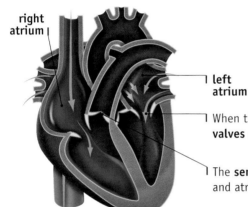

right atrium

left atrium

DIASTOLE

Diastole is marked by generalized dilation of the heart. In this phase, blood from the veins enters the atria.

When the heart is at rest, the **atrioventricular valves** are open.

The **semilunar valves** are closed during diastole and atrial systole.

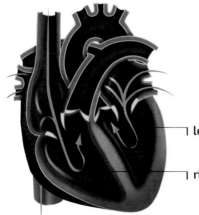

left ventricle

right ventricle

ATRIAL SYSTOLE

When the atria contract, they expel the blood they contain through the atrioventricular valves and into the ventricles. This first muscular contraction is called **atrial systole**. It fills the ventricles to 70 percent of their capacity.

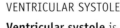

aorta

pulmonary trunk

VENTRICULAR SYSTOLE

Ventricular systole is the contraction of the ventricles. The atrioventricular valves close to keep blood from flowing back into the atria, while the semilunar valves open to let blood flow into the pulmonary trunk and aorta.

The contraction of the ventricles closes the **atrioventricular valves**.

Blood pressure forces the **semilunar valves** open.

CARDIAC CONDUCTION

Although nervous or hormonal messages can change the cardiac rhythm, the heart's rhythm is mainly dictated by certain cells in the myocardium that have the capacity to depolarize spontaneously and, thus, emit electrical impulses. This electrical stimulation propagates throughout the entire myocardium and triggers, first, the contraction of the atria and, next, the contraction of the ventricles. These essential cells depolarize, on average, every .8 second, causing the heart to beat 70 to 80 times per minute.

The sinoatrial node **❶**, located in the wall of the right atrium, is where cardiac excitation, or electrical stimulation of the myocardium, begins. When this node's cells depolarize, they create the electrical action potential that transmits a nerve impulse. By propagating rapidly from one cell to the next via the internodal tracts **❷**, the nerve impulse causes contraction of the atria. When it reaches the atrioventricular node **❸**, the impulse passes through the bundle of His **❹**, also called the atrioventricular bundle, which is the electrical conduit between the atria and the ventricles. The nerve impulse then descends along the interventricular septum to the apex of the heart and propagates rapidly through the muscle mass of the ventricles via the Purkinje network **❺**, causing the ventricles to contract about .16 seconds after the atria.

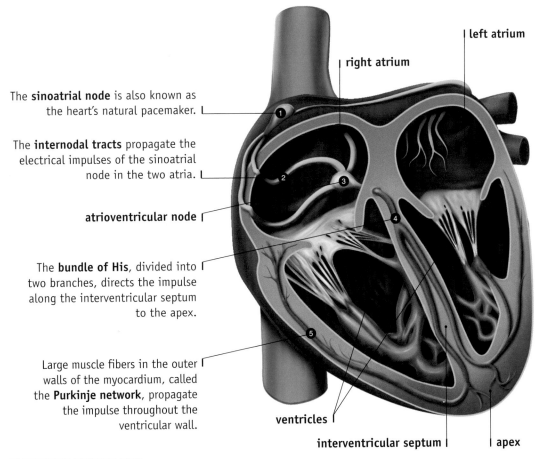

The **sinoatrial node** is also known as the heart's natural pacemaker.

The **internodal tracts** propagate the electrical impulses of the sinoatrial node in the two atria.

atrioventricular node

The **bundle of His**, divided into two branches, directs the impulse along the interventricular septum to the apex.

Large muscle fibers in the outer walls of the myocardium, called the **Purkinje network**, propagate the impulse throughout the ventricular wall.

left atrium

right atrium

ventricles

interventricular septum

apex

ELECTROCARDIOGRAMS

The electrocardiograph is an apparatus that uses sensors placed on the skin to measure the intensity of electrical currents resulting from depolarization of the heart's muscular fibers. The graph of the results, an electrocardiogram, shows the various deflections—known as deflections P, Q, R, S, and T—that correspond to the different phases of the cardiac cycle.

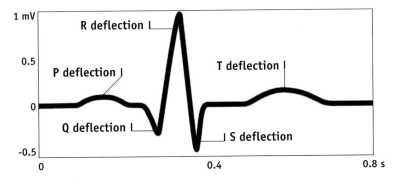

R deflection

P deflection

Q deflection

T deflection

S deflection

The **P deflection** indicates atrial depolarization, which leads to contraction of the atria. It is followed by the **QRS sequence**, corresponding to depolarization of the ventricles. The **T deflection** represents ventricular repolarization, which occurs immediately after contraction of the ventricles.

The Lymphatic System

Drainage and cleansing of the body's fluids

The lymphatic system is closely connected to the cardiovascular system. Plasma constantly leaks out of the blood capillaries and accumulates in the tissues. This leaked plasma is called interstitial fluid, better known as lymph. Through its network of vessels, the lymphatic system drains this fluid from the body, thus keeping the tissues from swelling. The lymph nodes remove infectious agents from the drained lymph and then the fluid is reintroduced into the cardiovascular system. The spleen is another organ that plays a cleansing role similar to that of the lymph nodes, though it does not process lymph directly.

DRAINAGE OF LYMPH

The lymphatic system is a one-way network that collects about 3 quarts (3 liters) of lymph per day from the body's various tissues. Lymph is evacuated from the interstitial space by the lymph capillaries and filtered through lymph nodes located in various places around the body. Then the filtered lymph flows into either the right lymphatic duct, which drains it from the upper right quarter of the body, or the thoracic duct, which receives filtered lymph from the rest of the organism. These two main canals join and open into the subclavian vein, through which the cleansed lymph returns to the cardiovascular system.

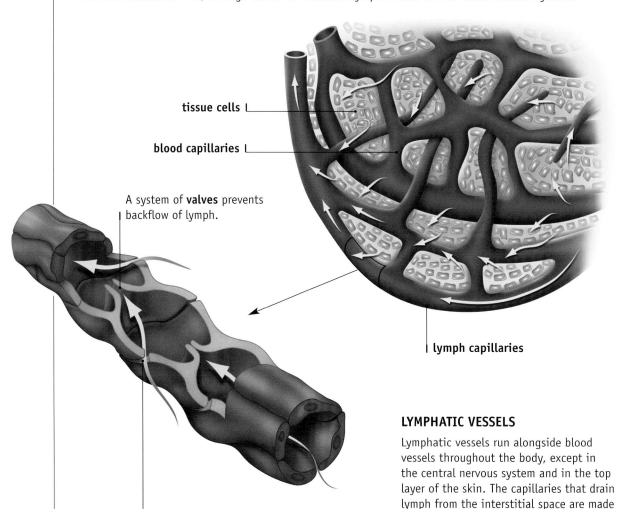

tissue cells

blood capillaries

A system of **valves** prevents backflow of lymph.

lymph capillaries

LYMPHATIC VESSELS

Lymphatic vessels run alongside blood vessels throughout the body, except in the central nervous system and in the top layer of the skin. The capillaries that drain lymph from the interstitial space are made of extremely thin, permeable membranes that allow interstitial fluid to penetrate them by simple pressure.

The **endothelial cells** of the lymph capillaries are very thin and easily permeable to interstitial liquid.

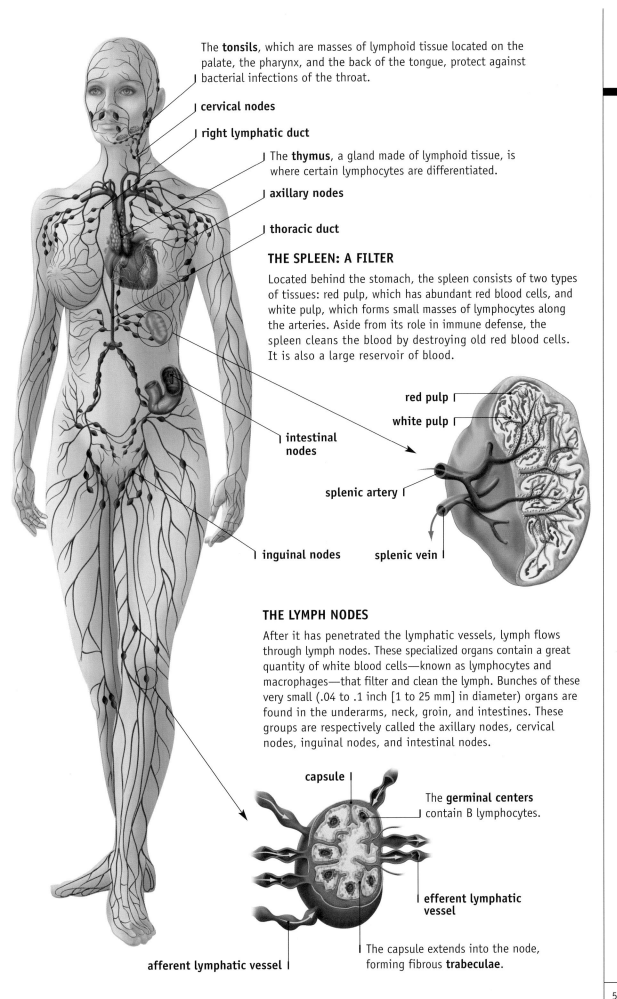

The **tonsils**, which are masses of lymphoid tissue located on the palate, the pharynx, and the back of the tongue, protect against bacterial infections of the throat.

cervical nodes

right lymphatic duct

The **thymus**, a gland made of lymphoid tissue, is where certain lymphocytes are differentiated.

axillary nodes

thoracic duct

THE SPLEEN: A FILTER

Located behind the stomach, the spleen consists of two types of tissues: red pulp, which has abundant red blood cells, and white pulp, which forms small masses of lymphocytes along the arteries. Aside from its role in immune defense, the spleen cleans the blood by destroying old red blood cells. It is also a large reservoir of blood.

red pulp

white pulp

intestinal nodes

splenic artery

inguinal nodes

splenic vein

THE LYMPH NODES

After it has penetrated the lymphatic vessels, lymph flows through lymph nodes. These specialized organs contain a great quantity of white blood cells—known as lymphocytes and macrophages—that filter and clean the lymph. Bunches of these very small (.04 to .1 inch [1 to 25 mm] in diameter) organs are found in the underarms, neck, groin, and intestines. These groups are respectively called the axillary nodes, cervical nodes, inguinal nodes, and intestinal nodes.

capsule

The **germinal centers** contain B lymphocytes.

efferent lymphatic vessel

afferent lymphatic vessel

The capsule extends into the node, forming fibrous **trabeculae**.

Immunity

How the body defends itself against infection

To protect itself against foreign bodies, the body has a number of complementary defense mechanisms. The epidermis, which functions as a physical barrier to bacteria and other pathogens, is backed up by tears, sebum, saliva, and gastric juices, all of which contain chemical defenses such as acids or enzymes. If a pathogen manages to break through this chemical line of defense, the body responds to the assault with an inflammatory reaction or a specific immune response. In both of these defenses against illness, white blood cells play a major role, reaching the infected region of the body through the blood and the lymphatic vessels and fighting off the invading pathogens and the cells they have affected.

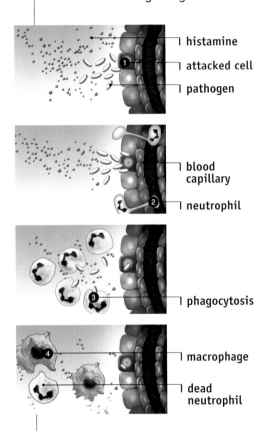

- histamine
- attacked cell
- pathogen
- blood capillary
- neutrophil
- phagocytosis
- macrophage
- dead neutrophil

THE INFLAMMATORY REACTION

When pathogens such as bacteria, viruses, or parasites invade the body, the region they attack reacts with a group of nonspecific defense mechanisms known as the inflammatory reaction.

After a cell is attacked ❶, a chain of chemical reactions takes place that results in the release of substances, such as histamine, that increase the diameter and permeability of nearby blood vessels. This change in the blood vessels causes the redness, heat, and swelling that is characteristic of an inflammation. The released substances also attract white blood cells to the site of the infection by a mechanism called chemotaxis. Neutrophils ❷ are the first white blood cells to appear; in less than one hour, they cross through the walls of the blood capillaries and begin destroying pathogens by phagocytosis ❸. They are joined by white blood cells called monocytes that transform into large cells called macrophages ❹. Macrophages continue destroying pathogens, as well as infected cells and dead neutrophils.

Where there is chronic inflammation, dead white blood cells and debris form pus, a yellowish liquid that accumulates in the wound. If pus is not eliminated quickly, it can form an abscess, which makes its dispersion even more difficult.

PHAGOCYTOSIS

Neutrophils, eosinophils, and monocytes are phagocytic cells—white blood cells capable of engulfing and digesting other cells. The process they perform, called phagocytosis, takes place in several steps. First, the phagocytic cell touches a pathogen with its pseudopods ❶. The foreign body is pulled toward the cell membrane of the phagocytic cell, which surrounds and engulfs it ❷. Lysosomes in the phagocytic cell adhere to the vesicle in which the pathogen is enclosed ❸, releasing enzymes that destroy the pathogen ❹. Residues of dead pathogens may either be used by or ejected out of the phagocytic cell.

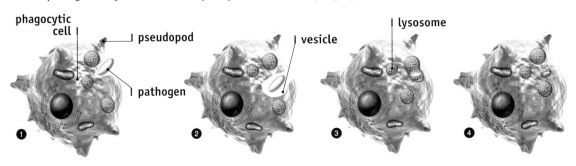

phagocytic cell

pseudopod

pathogen

vesicle

lysosome

❶ ❷ ❸ ❹

SPECIFIC IMMUNE RESPONSES

The inflammatory reaction is sometimes insufficient to fight the pathogens attacking the body. In such cases, the inflammatory reaction must be complemented by the specific immune responses, known as the cellular immune response and the humoral immune response.

THE CELLULAR IMMUNE RESPONSE

Pathogens ❶ that enter the body are attacked by macrophages ❷. Unlike neutrophils, macrophages do not completely digest the cells they envelop but decompose them into fragments of proteins that they incorporate into their membranes. These cells remain infected. T lymphocytes with receptors specific to the protein fragments in cell membranes react by becoming active and multiplying. Auxiliary T lymphocytes ❸ secrete cytokines, substances that stimulate the immune response. Cytotoxic T lymphocytes ❹ move to the site of the infection, where they attack the cells infected by the pathogen ❺.

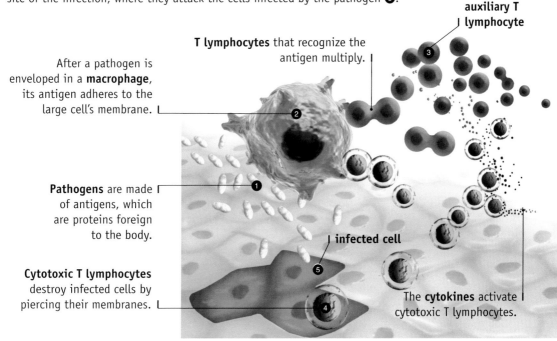

After a pathogen is enveloped in a **macrophage**, its antigen adheres to the large cell's membrane.

T lymphocytes that recognize the antigen multiply.

auxiliary T lymphocyte

Pathogens are made of antigens, which are proteins foreign to the body.

infected cell

Cytotoxic T lymphocytes destroy infected cells by piercing their membranes.

The **cytokines** activate cytotoxic T lymphocytes.

THE HUMORAL IMMUNE RESPONSE

In the presence of an antigen, B lymphocytes also multiply. These lymphocytes differentiate into plasma cells ❶, or cells capable of secreting antibodies. Antibodies ❷ act in different ways against pathogens. Some cause microbes to clump and be destroyed by phagocytic cells ❸. Others attach to antigens and attract certain groups of proteins, known as their complements ❹. Complement proteins pierce the cell membranes of pathogens and make them explode ❺.

During immune reactions, some T and B lymphocytes differentiate into long-lived cells, called memory cells, that retain a memory of the antigen that activated them. The presence of memory cells in the body greatly accelerates the immune response if there is a new infection by the same pathogen.

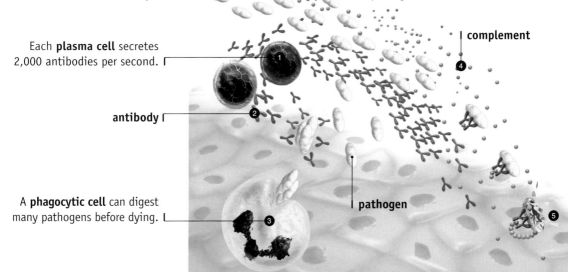

Each **plasma cell** secretes 2,000 antibodies per second.

complement

antibody

A **phagocytic cell** can digest many pathogens before dying.

pathogen

The Endocrine System

Hormones: the body's chemical messengers

The human body secretes and circulates around 50 different hormones. Hormones are chemical substances secreted into the blood system in order to circulate throughout the body and activate target cells. The wide variety of hormones is produced by endocrine cells, most of which are located in glands. The endocrine system, which is tightly linked to the nervous system, produces hormones that control many of the body's functions, including metabolism, homeostasis, growth, sexual maturation, and contraction of the smooth and cardiac muscles.

THE ENDOCRINE GLANDS

The endocrine system is composed of nine specialized glands—the pituitary, the thyroid, the four parathyroids, the two adrenals, and the thymus—and a number of organs capable of producing hormones, including the pancreas, heart, kidneys, ovaries, testicles, and intestines. The hypothalamus, which is not a gland but a nerve center, also plays a major role in the synthesis and release of hormonal factors.

Unlike substances produced by exocrine glands, which flow to their targets through ducts, hormones are released directly into the space surrounding the cells that secrete them. The very large number of blood vessels in endocrine glands enables hormones they secrete to spread throughout the blood system through the capillaries. Some homones circulate freely in the blood, while others must attach to carrier proteins in order to reach the target cells they activate.

Generally considered the master endocrine gland, the **pituitary** secretes 10 different hormones. Some of these substances then act on the other endocrine glands.

The **adrenal glands**, one of which is located above each kidney, have two distinct parts. The adrenal cortex secretes cortical hormones such as aldosterone and cortisol, as well as male sex hormones, or androgens, and female sex hormones, or estrogens. The adrenal medulla mainly produces adrenaline and noradrenaline, the hormones that are involved in the body's response to stressful stimuli.

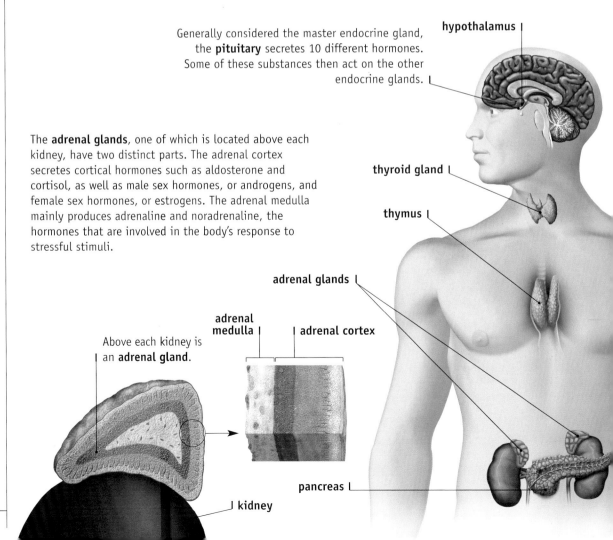

hypothalamus

thyroid gland

thymus

adrenal glands

adrenal medulla | | adrenal cortex

Above each kidney is an **adrenal gland**.

pancreas

kidney

THE THYROID GLAND

The thyroid gland—composed of two lobes, one on either side of the larynx—is activated by thyroid stimulating hormone (TSH). TSH is secreted by the pituitary gland. The hormones secreted by the thyroid gland itself, commonly called T3 and T4, are made from iodine, and their main task is to regulate growth and metabolism.

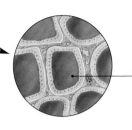

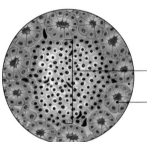

Thyroid hormones are stored in tiny sacs called **thyroid follicles.**

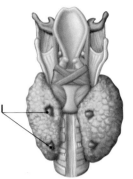

The **parathyroid glands,** located behind the thyroid gland, make parathyroid hormone, which controls the calcium level in the body.

trachea

thyroid gland

THE PANCREAS

The pancreas plays an important role in digestion by producing enzymes, and it is also part of the endocrine system. Groups of cells in the pancreas called islets of Langerhans secrete four different hormones that regulate the glucose level in the body. The most important of these hormones are glucagon and insulin.

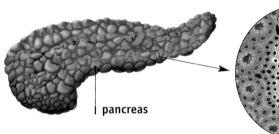

The **islets of Langerhans** are the cells responsible for endocrine activity in the pancreas.

The **acini** are groups of cells responsible for exocrine production of pancreatic enzymes.

pancreas

HOW HORMONES WORK

When a hormone diffuses outside a capillary, it can act on a target cell, or a cell with receptors that correspond to it. There are two ways that hormones work on target cells. On one hand, steroid hormones ❶ enter a target cell directly through its cell membrane. They then unite with receptor proteins inside the target cell's nucleus, either stimulating or blocking the cell's genetic activity. Protein hormones ❷, on the other hand, cannot penetrate target cells. They attach to the target cell's membrane, and this attachment activates a receptor that releases a messenger within the cell.

Each target cell has between 5,000 and 100,000 **hormone receptors** on its surface. The number of receptors may be reduced or increased to adapt to the quantity of hormones in the blood.

Hormones belong to different classes of chemical substances, including steroids (testosterone), proteins (insulin), polypeptides (parathyroid hormone), and derivatives of amino acids (adrenaline).

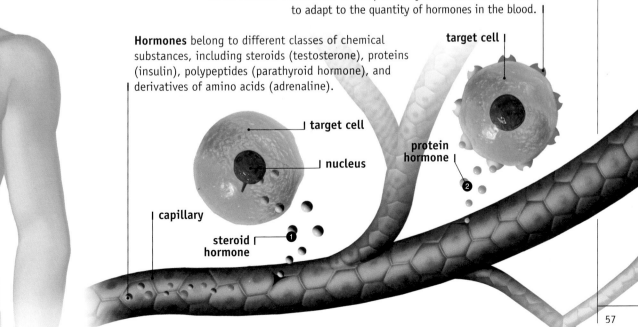

target cell

target cell

nucleus

protein hormone ❷

capillary

steroid hormone ❶

The Hypothalamus and the Pituitary Gland

The control centers of the endocrine system

Because it controls the activity of a number of other glands, the pituitary gland is often considered the main gland of the endocrine system. The pituitary gland itself, however, is controlled by the hypothalamus, a nerve center that is involved in the regulation of many vital functions. Between these two important structures, the hypothalamus and the pituitary gland produce one-third of all the hormones in the body. These hormones influence bodily functions ranging from lactation and urine retention to skin pigmentation and bone growth.

THE HYPOTHALAMUS

Located under the thalamus, the hypothalamus is the part of the brain that is composed of several nuclei that control the autonomic nervous system. This system regulates hunger, thirst, body temperature, and sleep. The hypothalamus also influences sexual behavior and the emotions of anger and fear. Closely linked to the pituitary gland, it acts as a coordinator between the nervous and endocrine systems.

THE PITUITARY GLAND

The pituitary gland is a mass about .5 inch (1.3 cm) in diameter located in a cavity in the sphenoid bone called the sella turcica. It is made of two different structures; the neurohypophysis, or posterior pituitary, contains the extensions of the secreting neurons of the hypothalamus, while the adenohypophysis, or anterior pituitary, is composed only of endocrine cells.

sphenoid bone

The **hypothalamus** contains a dozen nervous nuclei.

pituitary gland

neurohypophysis | adenohypophysis

ACTIVITY OF THE THYROID GLAND: AN EXAMPLE OF HORMONAL FEEDBACK CONTROL

The production of thyroid hormones by the thyroid gland is regulated by a chain of hormonal stimulations. First, the hypothalamus ❶ secretes thyrotropin-releasing hormone (TRH), which travels through the capillary network to stimulate the adenohypophysis ❷. The adenohypophysis reacts by releasing thyrotropin, or thyroid-stimulating hormone (TSH), which, in turn, activates the production of thyroid hormones by the thryroid gland ❸.

This mechanism is controlled by a feedback system. If nerve receptors detect signs of too high a concentration of thyroid hormones in the body, production of TRH by the hypothalamus is inhibited. Receiving less stimulation, the pituitary gland reduces secretion of thyrotropin, which, in turn, reduces the secretions of the thyroid gland. This process is called negative feedback. In contrast, if there is not enough of a thyroid hormone in the body, feedback to the hypothalamus stops, and it then releases TRH.

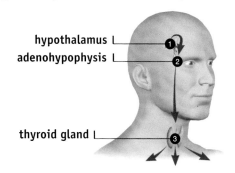

hypothalamus
adenohypophysis

thyroid gland

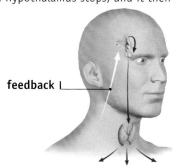

feedback

ADENOHYPOPHYSIC HORMONES

Controlled by the hypothalamus via a capillary network, the adenohypophysis secretes six different hormones: adrenocorticotropic hormone (ACTH), thyrotropin (TSH), prolactin, growth hormone, follicle-stimulating hormone (FSH), and luteinizing hormone (LH).

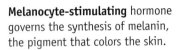

The axons of the **secreting neurons** of the hypothalamus route the hormones vasopressin and oxytocin to the neurohypophysis.

nervous nucleus

Melanocyte-stimulating hormone governs the synthesis of melanin, the pigment that colors the skin.

Thyrotropin governs the secretion of hormones by the thyroid gland.

NEUROHYPOPHYSIC HORMONES

The secreting cells of the hypothalamus synthesize and secrete the hormones vasopressin and oxytocin, which are released into the blood system by the neurohypophysis.

Prolactin triggers and controls the synthesis of milk by the mammary glands.

neurohypophysis | | adenohypophysis

Vasopressin makes the kidneys reduce the quantity of urine excreted, provokes constriction of arterioles, and reduces perspiration.

The adrenal cortices, which make cortisol, the substance that regulates the storage of glucose, are stimulated by **adrenocorticotropic hormone**.

Growth hormone is the main pituitary hormone. This protein stimulates general body growth and affects metabolism.

Oxytocin provokes uterine contractions during childbirth and triggers the release of breast milk.

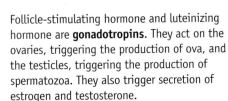

Follicle-stimulating hormone and luteinizing hormone are **gonadotropins**. They act on the ovaries, triggering the production of ova, and the testicles, triggering the production of spermatozoa. They also trigger secretion of estrogen and testosterone.

The Urinary System
How the kidneys filter the blood

Water, which constitutes 60 percent of the weight of the human body, circulates mainly in the bloodstream, carrying nutrients and waste. The urinary system allows the body's volume of water to be controlled and certain substances to be eliminated. The kidneys function as filters by extracting waste materials from the blood without depriving it of nutritive elements. The urine produced by the kidneys is stored in the bladder and then evacuated through the urethra. To make up for this loss of liquid through urination, an adult must drink 2 quarts (2 liters) of water per day.

THE ORGANS OF THE URINARY SYSTEM

Located on either side of the aorta and the inferior vena cava, the kidneys are supplied with blood by the renal arteries. They filter this blood and produce urine, which is transported to the bladder by the two ureters. The urethra, which carries urine out of the bladder, is longer in men than in women.

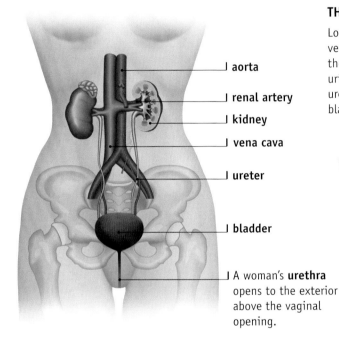

- aorta
- renal artery
- kidney
- vena cava
- ureter
- bladder
- A woman's **urethra** opens to the exterior above the vaginal opening.

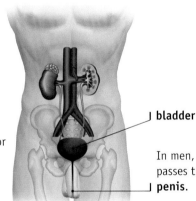

- bladder

In men, the urethra passes through the **penis**.

THE BLADDER

Before being eliminated, urine is temporarily stored in the bladder. This sac made of muscle tissue is spherical in shape when it is full and flat when it is empty. The bladder can hold up to an average of 17 ounces (500 ml), but the urination reflex appears when the bladder contains between 7 and 14 ounces (200 and 400 ml) of urine. The detrusor muscle contracts while the internal sphincter relaxes, leading to evacuation of urine through the urethra. The external urethral sphincter, which is voluntarily controlled, allows urination to be blocked.

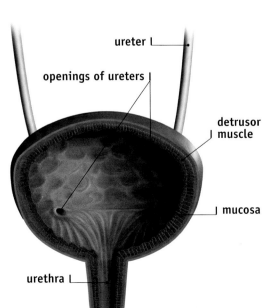

- ureter
- openings of ureters
- detrusor muscle
- mucosa
- urethra

empty bladder   **full bladder**

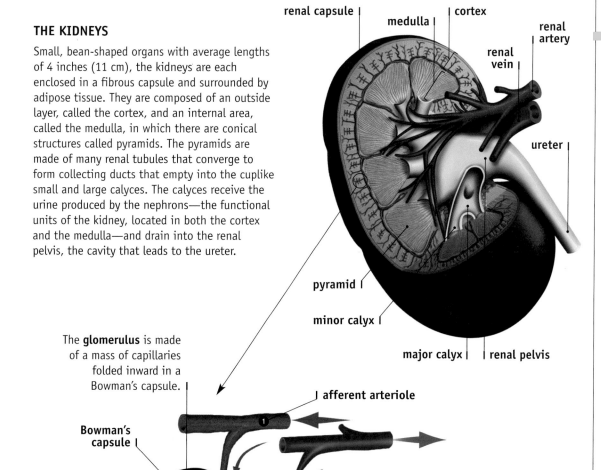

THE KIDNEYS

Small, bean-shaped organs with average lengths of 4 inches (11 cm), the kidneys are each enclosed in a fibrous capsule and surrounded by adipose tissue. They are composed of an outside layer, called the cortex, and an internal area, called the medulla, in which there are conical structures called pyramids. The pyramids are made of many renal tubules that converge to form collecting ducts that empty into the cuplike small and large calyces. The calyces receive the urine produced by the nephrons—the functional units of the kidney, located in both the cortex and the medulla—and drain into the renal pelvis, the cavity that leads to the ureter.

renal capsule | | medulla | | cortex
renal artery
renal vein |
ureter |

pyramid [

minor calyx [

major calyx | | renal pelvis

The **glomerulus** is made of a mass of capillaries folded inward in a Bowman's capsule. |

| afferent arteriole

Bowman's capsule |

The renal tubule descends into the medulla, where it forms a **loop of Henle**.

| efferent arteriole

filtrate |

| peritubular capillaries

| renal tubule

Collecting ducts receive the urine made in many renal tubules.

Urine is 90 percent water, but it also contains urea, creatinine, uric acid, and ions.

NEPHRONS: FROM BLOOD TO URINE

Each kidney contains about 1 million nephrons, or units that filter the blood and produce urine. Blood enters a nephron through an afferent arteriole ❶ that subdivides into numerous capillaries to form a glomerulus ❷, which is a small sphere enveloped in a Bowman's capsule. Some of the constituent elements of blood, including water, mineral salts, and glucose, pass through the walls of the capillaries and form a liquid called filtrate ❸. The capillaries come together again in an efferent arteriole ❹, which leaves the glomerulus. The filtrate enters a renal tubule ❺, which winds through the cortex and the medulla of the kidney, exchanging substances with peritubular capillaries ❻. These exchanges enable the blood to reabsorb some useful products. It is estimated that out of 190 quarts (180 liters) of filtrate produced every day, about 189 quarts (179 liters) are reabsorbed. What remains of the filtrate becomes urine ❼, which is drained toward the calyces through the collecting ducts.

Glossary

adipose tissue: A type of connective tissue formed mainly of fat cells.

amino acid: The type of organic compound that is the basic structural unit of proteins.

antibody: A soluble protein that attaches to a specific foreign substance and helps to destroy it.

antigen: A foreign substance that causes an antibody to react when it is introduced into an organism.

articulate: To join with in such a way as to allow motion between the parts.

carcinogenic: Causing or tending to cause cancer.

cartilage: Strong semi-opaque connective tissue composed of chondrocytes covered with a dense network of collagen and elastic fibers.

chemotaxis: Movement toward or away from a chemical stimulus.

cortex: The outer layer of a bodily organ or structure.

cuboidal: Resembling a cube in shape.

dexterity: Skill in using the hands.

enzyme: Protein that acts as a catalyst for a chemical reaction.

fiber: A substance made of a large number of filaments; the main component of certain tissues.

filiform: Threadlike.

genetic: Having to do with genes and heredity.

helical: Shaped in a spiral.

hemorrhage: A large discharge of blood.

homeostasis: The tendency of an organism to maintain a stable internal state.

hyaline: Resembling glass.

intracellular: Within a cell.

intrinsic muscle: A muscle contained entirely within an organ or a part of the body.

lipid: The type of organic, water-insoluble substance that makes up fatty matter.

matrix: The homogeneous intercellular substance in all tissues.

membrane: A thin layer of tissue.

metabolic: Related to the physical processes in an organism by which it produces its substance and makes energy available within the body.

molecule: A particle formed of two or more atoms.

organ: A part of the body made up of various kinds of tissues that has a definite shape and performs a particular function.

pathogen: A disease-producing agent, such as a bacterium or virus.

perfusion: Passing through blood or lymphatic vessels to an organ or tissue.

pigment: A substance that produces color in a tissue.

pore: A small opening in a membrane or the skin.

propagate: To travel through a substance or space.

protein: An organic substance made of long chains of amino acids, found in abundance in living matter.

renal: Having to do with the kidneys.

sinus: A cavity inside a bone.

solutes: Substances dissolved in a liquid.

stem cell: An immature cell capable of multiplying indefinitely and differentiating into all cell types in the human body.

stimulus: Environmental element capable of activating a sensory receptor.

template: A strand of DNA that serves as a pattern for the formation of another complementary strand

trabecula: A fine cord of connective tissue extending within an organ and supporting it.

vascularized: Having blood vessels or other fluid-carrying vessels or ducts.

viscera: The organs in the body's cavities, especially those in the abdomen.

Books

Atlas of the Human Body. Takeo Takahashi (Harper Collins)

The Big Idea: Crick, Watson, and DNA. Paul Strathern (Anchor Books)

Body (Secret Worlds). Richard Walker (DK Publishing)

Eyewitness: The Human Body. Steve Parker (DK Publishing)

The Heart and the Circulatory System. Carol Ballard (Raintree/Steck Vaughn)

How the Circulatory System Works. Robert E. Mehler (Blackwell Science, Inc.)

How the Endocrine System Works. J. Matthew Neal (Blackwell Science, Inc.)

How the Immune System Works. Lauren M. Sompayrac (Blackwell Science, Inc.)

The Immune System (21st Century Health and Wellness). Edward Edelson (Chelsea House)

Incredible Voyage: Exploring the Human Body. (National Geographic Society)

The Skeletal System (Human Body System). Alvin Silverstein, Virginia Silverstein, Robert Silverstein (Twenty First Century Books)

Videos and CD-ROMs

Blood and the Circulatory System (CD-ROM). (Library Video)

Cells. (Discovery Channel School)

The DNA Revolution. (The History Channel)

Glands and Hormones: Vol. 2 (Body Atlas). (Library Video)

Interactive Human Body (Mega Systems Interactive Series) (CD-ROM). (Library Video)

The Magic of Cells. (Library Video)

The Musculoskeletal System (Just the Facts Learning Series). (Just the Facts)

Web Sites

BBC Science Sites: Human Body
www.bbc.co.uk/science/humanbody/enhanced/index.shtml

Cells Alive!
www.cellsalive.com

The Heart: An Online Exploration
sln.fi.edu/biosci/heart.html

The Interactive Skeleton
www.eskeletons.org/viewer/humanSelect.html

Index